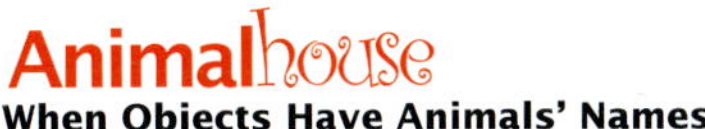

Animalhouse
When Objects Have Animals' Names

Printed in Italy
ISBN 88-8158-401-8

Edizioni della Triennale

Fondazione La Triennale di Milano
viale Alemagna 6
20121 Milano
tel. +39-0272434.1
fax +39-0289010693
www.triennale.it

Edizioni Charta
Via della Moscova 27
20121 Milano
tel +39-026598098/026598200
fax +39-026598577
email: edcharta@tin.it
www.chartaartbooks.it

Permanent Collection of Italian Design

Animalhouse
When Objects Have Animals' Names

Palazzo della Triennale
Viale Alemagna 6, Milano
10 May – 8 September 2002

Curator
Silvana Annicchiarico

Exhibition Installation
Giancarlo Basili

Graphic Project
Daniele Mastrapasqua

Organization
Elisa Testori

Setting-up
Luigi Cappelletti
Tosetto Allestimenti
Decoration by Gianni Pellegrini
Lighthing by Marzoratimpianti

Thanks to **ABET LAMINATI**

Cover
Topolino 500
Dante Giacosa, 1936, Fiat

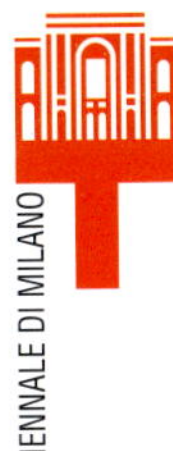

PERMANENT COLLECTION OF ITALIAN DESIGN

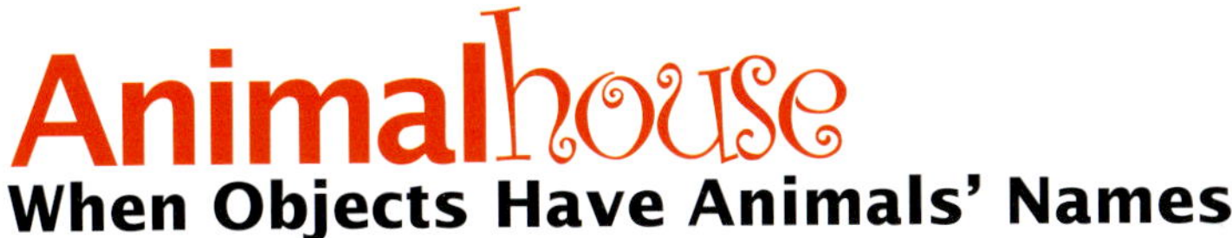

Animalhouse
When Objects Have Animals' Names

edited by Silvana Annicchiarico

CHARTA

Milan Triennale Foundation

Board of Directors
Aldo Bassetti
Renato Besana
Roberto Cecchi
Silvia Corinaldi Rusconi Clerici
Patrizia Grieco
Augusto Morello, *President*
Giuseppe Panza di Biumo
Davide Rampello

Auditors' Committee
Stefano Coppa
Antonio Durante
Alfredo Giacomazzi
Adriana Rampinelli, *President*
Domenico Salerno

General Affairs Sector
Federica Molteni
Annunciata Marinella Alberghina
Franco Romeo

Activities Sector
Laura Agnesi
Roberta Sommariva

Library, Documentation, Archives Sector
Ferruccio Dilda

Technical Administrative Services Sector
Stefano Arrigo
Alessandro Cammarata
Giuseppina Di Vito
Marina Gerosa
Isabella Micieli
Franco Olivucci
Pierantonio Ramaioli

Curator of the Permanent Collection of Italian Design
Silvana Annicchiarico

Scientific Collaboration
Silvana Annicchiarico
Design
Luca Molinari
Architecture
Raimonda Riccini
Fashion

Producer
Roberto Bucci

Press Office
Antonella La Seta Catamancio

Contents

The names of design and the design of names

Augusto Morello
President of the Triennale di Milano

This is the second exploration of the significance of names in the practice of contemporary design: its predecessor examined the names of women, and now the names of animals provide the focus.

A name may be assigned to a genotype or a phenotype – the genotype "large lorry" may be a "Bison" (of the highway), the phenotype "ad hoc lamp" may be a "Tizio" – but assigning a name to an object for personal use is generally equivalent to a confession made by the designer and/or manufacturer. For the user it is only a convention of identification, though more stimulating than the mere numbers that businesses once assigned to items in their product portfolio.

Any name, however, always offers a proposed interpretation. Even more so when one is dealing with a "standard type," and particularly when – as often happens – the name is that of an animal whose characteristics and behavior are generally well-known, or indicate some particular quality. "Generally," because they are rarely close to the reality: animals – especially from Disney onwards – may be loved, petted and cuddled by children (or sentimental grown-ups) because of their sweetness and sympathy; and often, therefore, they are impostors.

Bears, kangaroos, hippopotamuses and even deer are not without their element of mischief and danger; for a mouse to be made likeable it has to be treated affectionately by calling it "little mouse" (or a bear, "baby bear").

So it becomes a stock animal, with a name that conveys a stock feeling or a stock emotion – in short, a kind of partially translated testimonial.

Those who recall the appearance of the *Topolino* (Little Mouse) before the war know that the name was not assigned by the manufacturer. The name of this first low-cost Italian car was invented by the users and only afterwards adopted by the general public, and also by the manufacturer. Immediately after the war, on the other hand, the manufacturer of the *Vespa* (Wasp) was not to be forestalled, and the name was, in a manner of speaking, imposed. The shape of the letter V in the logo also betrayed the inspiration for the rounded shape of the rear of the vehicle, which resembles an insect's abdomen. In this respect the *Vespa* revealed a formalistic feature that found a contrast later in the *Lambretta*, with its visible structure almost devoid of "bodywork" (and therefore preferred by strict rationalists), the name of which came from the place where the manufacturer's tube factory was located.

But the resultant general adoption of the name *Vespa* was probably due to the aggressive quality of an animal that in itself enjoys little sympathy: for Italians the *Vespa* was an aggressive instrument of work and competitiveness, at a time when the per capita income was too low to allow widespread acquisition of four-wheeled vehicles.

When a variant of the *Vespa* was translated into a vehicle for moving goods, it was called the *Ape* (Bee), with a more sympathetic, beneficent quality, though equally hardworking. But perhaps there was more to it: the *Vespa* buzzes, and the success of the name might have been due to a negative premonition of the future noise level in a city besieged by motors.

From this, one might draw the conclusion that the success of a name depends much more on conscious or unconscious factors of interpretation, which users and society evoke in adopting it.

Although the case of the *Vespa* may seem anomalous – because animal names are usually assigned to objects "positively" (in other words, with a view to *captatio benevolentiae*) – those with the role of assigning added value to design cannot deny that the name assigned to a product nevertheless forms part of the complex of knowledge and experience directed at driving prices higher than those obtainable for functionality alone. Names can thus form part of a design based on mere promotion, by which the (often false) quality of the animal is transferred to the fetish/object.

It remains to be seen whether this becomes true only at the point when communication takes command, and whether it is always true: both in the sense that even a genuinely innovative design may be embellished with some name or other, and in the sense that the attribution of a name is always an indication of "lesser" design.

Olivetti adopted names endowed with meaning (replacing the earlier *M1*, *M20*, etc.) in the years leading up to the war (with the *Studio*, Marcello Nizzoli's first contribution) and in the post-war period, with *Lexicon* and *Lettera*, *Summa* and *Divisumma*, *Diaspron* and *Tetraktys*, all by Nizzoli; and then later *Programma*, *Logos* and others by Mario Bellini. They were all names coined by Franco Fortini, and in them one could read the aim of conferring cultural nobility upon the functions of the machine; even if, in some cases, the name often became the pretext for a promotional slogan – but always one of high quality, being devised by Fortini himself ("Lettera: as light as a syllable, as complete as a sentence"). How different was the choice of the name *Valentine*, with its echoes of Guido Crepax? There had been a change in the very perspective of design – a type of design with formal variants to be communicated swiftly – but, as is well known, in this case without particular success beyond that of the intellectual myth, for many technical and market-related reasons.

In this sense, the "greater" or "lesser" quality of design seems to be related to the strategy of names. It is the same with many examples from the collection "animal house" that is now offered for reflection to those who seek to study the clues and adventures of a complex and fascinating history.

Animal morphological sources in the design of spaces and objects for dwellings

Gianni Ottolini
Politecnico di Milano

1. Iconic sources of forms

If one considers form in architecture and design products solely in terms of how it presents itself to sensory perception, leaving aside both the ways in which it is constructed and the utility that one can obtain from it, the figurative references or "iconic sources" to which it can be traced back universally are manifold.

Apart from "abstract" sources, which employ the expressive values of figuration, measurement, position, texture, lighting, coloring, etc., together with suggestions taken from inorganic nature (Gio Ponti's "architecture is a crystal"), and also sources derived from "historic styles," from languages already experimented with in the past, one can recognize another major source for the forms of architecture and objects and their decoration, understood as an expressive emphasis that makes their identity and meaning more precise: a "naturalistic" source, the figurative theme of which is explicitly a living object taken from nature (a flower, tree, animal or person) in one of the infinite formal facets, and also alterations, with which it can be translated into work.

International Style, breaking away from historic styles which had been emptied of meaning by the eclecticism of the late nineteenth century, and from the Art Nouveau which had immediately preceded it, put forward a new abstract code for the specification and equipping of living spaces, with Mies van der Rohe correcting the rediscovered simplicity of geometrical figures with the emphasis given to the intrinsic (but still abstract) decorative values of the materials employed. It thus became intimately associated with the avant-gardes of painting, poetry and music of the turn of the century, which took issue with the historicist or naturalistic references of traditional languages and were focused entirely on the pure expressiveness of their artistic resources.

Today, a different critical condition makes us still recognize a contemporary message in Morris's *Strawberry Thief* chintz of 1883, with lively little birds set behind a dense tangle of branches and flowers, or the bucrania and ribbons proposed by Michelangelo in the early sixteenth century for the floor and ceiling of the Biblioteca Laurenziana, or the gigantic "bacteria" of plastic laminate designed by Ettore Sottsass.

2. Organic forms

In contrast to "analytical" forms, derived from the assembly of constituent elements or parts recognizable by their outline, which becomes a joint or line of connection (as in a rustic wood and straw chair, where the slats and crossbars are quite different parts that are jointed together, with external lines visible; or in a building system with prefabricated components left showing), a "synthetic" form, or an "organic" form (so called by analogy to the "skin" of an animal, which continuously covers all the internal organs), is one in which the parts are not recognizable as figures but are plastic contractions, dilations or distortions of a continuous, homogeneous material (as in Saarinen's celebrated "egg-like" chair, actually consisting of two pieces, each of a different material, unified by their profile and color, in which the "bowl" of the chair bends to form the back and arms without discontinuity; or in many forms poured in cement, or stamped in steel or plastic).

One should note the ability of finishing and decorative treatments to change – from analytical to organic and vice versa – the style of a formal arrangement derived only from constructional factors: in armchairs of the baroque period, the operation of turning whole parts out of wood introduced the discontinuity of prism-shaped figures (where the parts are inserted into one another) and rounded figures (along the body, where there are no joints), in accordance with a prevailing analytical formal aim; in rococo armchairs, the connection of discontinuous parts made of wood (the legs and rails) is made "organic" not only by the continuous, flowing, geometrical form of the external and internal profiles but also by the gilding and lacquering of the surface, covering up any joints. The same could be said in architecture, in relation to the general unifying role of plasterwork and paintwork, and the distinguishing role of friezes and plinths, cornices and mouldings. From this strictly morphological viewpoint, "organic form" is not strictly referable to an immediate naturalistic iconic reference that makes the appearance of some specific living thing recognizable in it.

But if we leave abstract morphology and consider the life contained and in some way "represented" in the forms of organic nature, and in those of animals in particular, and the part that those forms have played in the configuration of spaces and objects in human dwellings from the most remote times to the present day, one enters a varied, complex, problematic territory that here can only be outlined.

3. Protodocuments

In French and Cantabrian caverns of forty thousand and twenty thousand years ago, in habitable spaces that were not constructed but found in nature, whole walls or vaults (as at Altamira) are painted with images of groups of animals, or battles with them, in colors of charcoal, ochre or red ochre. They represent the first real "theatre of consciousness" of the dramas of the individual and, above all, the collective liberation of mankind.

Dino Formaggio writes: "...it is a population of hunters: they know animals, animals are their life...they have the animal before them as if they were wrestling together. It's a necessity, food...but also it is something different, the deadly enemy, the terrifying master, or slave. Palaeolithic man seeks freedom from the animal through mastery over the animal, in this case by magic and painting; and he represents all this in a fight that is one of men against animals and vice-versa; but also of animals against animals, as possible totemic figures of different clans fighting amongst themselves... Sociopolitical struggles, fighting for power and fighting for life, fighting for mastery over animals and over the world of objects by means of techniques of magic ritual and instruments and arms... In this furious, savage intersection of magic powers and violent sexual, cognitive and social oppositions, between the roaming of the human hunters and the herds, the hand printed by the artist directly on the cave wall acquires all its meaning, either as a sign of magic powers of mastery, a typical instrument of ritual evocation, or as a module of composition that directly senses and applies the golden section..."

Passing from prehistoric to historical times, we can only jot down a few flashes of memory: the Mycenean Lion Gate, a typical passageway space for the security of the dwelling, with two symmetrical animals watching over the central stele that perhaps was in charge of a sacred object; Tutankhamen's bed with its stylized, elongated sides representing two sacred cows with their horns arched in a circle; the rites of the founding of cities among the Romans, described by Joseph Rykwert, wherein the person who set about founding a city or a military barracks, in order to ascertain whether the place and the time were propitious or not, had previously questioned the flight of the birds, the displacements of roaming animals, the thundering and movements of the clouds, and above all had verified the satisfactory state of the liver of sacrificed animals that had been grazing in those places; and also the delightful naturalistic scenes painted on Roman walls, or the bad-tempered cur of the "cave canem" (beware of dog) depicted in mosaic on the floor of the entrance to the House of the Faun in Pompeii.

By this time generally confident and tame, the animal in the world of the classical Greeks and Romans, with its appearance and nature, remained a constant object of comparison for individual and social behavior, and especially a model of reference for artistic creation. Direct experience and repeated observation of nature – in its forms and in the living forces that seemed to animate it, and with which one was constantly confronted – was for centuries the fundamental poetic principle of "mimesis" (imitation). With this, the consciousness of individuals and collective society periodically celebrated not the exorcism of unknown or hostile forces, but above all a balanced coexistence of humans and the environment in which they lived.

In architecture and in all the other arts, it was the different ontological and eschatological perspective of Christian thought that carried out a hierarchical reordering of the relationships between people, animals, trees and things, directing them towards their Creator as a unique focus of animation and of any possible significance.

4. The first modern writer of treatises (in Latin)

After the significant symbolic presences of animals in the representations of Christian art, from the lamb myths in the Byzantine mosaics in the Mausoleum of Galla Placidia to the monstrous gryphons of gothic gargoyles (which had an extraordinary Art Nouveau revival in the Gaudí of the "dragon's back" that covers the Casa Batlló, as well as the symbolic forest of the Sagrada Familia) the classical naturalistic idea returned in the age of humanism.

In Leon Battista Alberti's treatise on architecture, in which the modern designer's predecessor is delineated as a cultured, responsible, independent individual, a structural similarity between a building and a living body is repeatedly put forward, in which the imitation of nature has to do not with external forms but with something more profound: "our ancestors…established that nature, the creator of the finest forms, should be their model.

Therefore they set about deriving the principles that in nature preside over the formation of things and applied them to their own methods of construction."

In his inquiry into the structural rules of beauty – which above all is "concinnitas" (from *cum-canere*, to sing together), in other words, the agreement and harmony of the parts within the whole – he maintains that "as in the animal organism, each limb is in harmony with the others; so in the building each part must harmonize with the others" in accordance with permanent numerical principles of dimensional relationship and placement. Even if more operative principles are suggested ("in imitation of nature, they never used odd numbers for the parts of the skeleton of the building, i.e., columns, corners, etc., because no animal exists that stands on an odd number of legs…"), nature is considered above all in its simplicity, consistency, and functionality in the formation of limbs – in other words, in its tendency to obtain the maximum aesthetic result with the minimum formal or economic complication. It is understood as living form, which "creates the beautiful in endless individual cases in which formal balance has behind it the miracle of life" (Portoghesi).

5. The modern animal machine

In the avant-gardes of design five hundred years later, organic nature, the source of all teaching, was uprooted and reabsorbed within the "lesson of the machine," characterized by the lucid rationality of solving problems rather than by their formal solutions. In Le Corbusier in the early twenties, the machine – a human creation – was considered as being "composed of organs that fulfil functions similar to natural phenomena...[it] sets before us sparkling disks, spheres and cylinders of polished steel...cut with a theoretical precision and a sharpness that nature never shows us" (1925).

This position, as Maria Lucia Cannarozzo has made clear, was based on the acquisition of the new science of life, nineteenth-century biology, which explained the conditions of existence of life itself in the diversity of its manifestations, describing in terms of comparative anatomy the invisible and solitary functioning of organs (for the purposes of breathing, movement, locomotion, reproduction, etc.) in the unity of each living body.

The theoretical scheme of the human body, broken down into three functional systems ("skeleton for carrying, muscles for acting, viscera for feeding and making it function") was, for Le Corbusier, the paradigm of reference both for the automobile ("frame, bodywork, engine") and for the house ("independent frame, external façade bringing light, internal dividers that freely define the internal spatial 'organs' of the dwelling, contact with the land and with the sky").

Thus, with a touch of rationalistic presumption that Le Corbusier himself corrected with the brutalist plasticism of the following decades, once again modern functionalism sets as the basis of the planning of architecture and the design of objects the intimate integration of function, construction and form present in nature, concealing its organicist source within the very metaphor of the "house as a machine for living in" (and not only in the more explicit definition of the house as a habitable "cell," solitary with the habitable organism – as the residential building is still described by the technological culture of planning – and with the urban "tissue" of which it forms a part).

The aesthetics derived from it did away with any "squandering": a single principle of refinement governed both "natural selection" and "mechanical selection."

6. An Italian master

Contrasting with the utilitarian conception of the machine – with its functionalist purism that had reduced forms to an abstract, calligraphic, geometrical expression within the closed rigidity of an unduly severe architectural code placed above nature – Carlo De Carli and the Italian organicism of the early forties confirmed the passion for "forms originated by the diagrams of the new age" under the banner of speed (Carlo Mollino's "twin torpedo" car), but considered them only a part of a single "great poetic fact, which is life in movement."

De Carli recalled the essential forms of airplanes and, at the same time, "the rapid, vibrant lines of antelopes, gazelles, great flying creatures, [and] the exact expression of movement" in fibers in tension, ready to react (yet "it is not a sensation of excitement, because anything full of strength is in perfect equilibrium, giving a sense of calm power"); and he translated them into the shapes of his furniture, with strong "bony" nodes of continuous connection between wooden structural elements.

The focus of attention was the "continuity" between architecture and nature: "In the infinite field of nature, no longer merely functional, where the precise functional premises inherent in nature itself exist... the architect can live fully, creating architecture that continues the work of nature itself without brusque interruptions, in perfect harmony with all natural forms."

Thus "the interior becomes a nucleus of life, no longer the physical void of an abstract object, motionless on the ground, but the spirit of the walls among which people circulate, with which the house lives among humans and plants... Every house comes into being spontaneously, following the movement that resonates where it gradually grows; a movement of divine and human colors, sounds, smells and images. It is not an object, but the continuation of all around it."

7. Two disciplinary settings

Even in the increasing divergence of the cultures of architecture and industrial design, two disciplinary settings now seem more capable of jointly developing the "analogical" method and feeling with which designers in the two sectors have traditionally referenced animal organisms.

Bionics, on the one hand, is the study of living or lifelike systems, working toward the discovery of new principles, techniques and processes to be applied in the planning of new technical systems and products. On a strictly figurative level, it works largely through geometrical abstraction and mathematization of bodies that are investigated in depth in terms of their three-dimensional details and the formal principles that structure them, to increase the possibilities of transferring them to analogous objects. Thus the shape of a whale, which does not require a high expenditure of energy, is transferred to the shape of a ship in order

to reduce its energy consumption; or the thermoscopic vision of a snake cross-
es over into infrared photography.

Environmental planning, on the other hand, perhaps in conjunction with bioengi-
neering, once again compares buildings with the bodies of animals, no longer fig-
uratively or in terms of geometrical or spatial/functional relationships, but con-
sidering them as genuine living organisms, increasingly endowed with control and
self-monitoring devices and sensors with "artificial intelligence," which interact not
only with variations in external environmental conditions but also with alterations
in the state of the body and the intentions of those who dwell in it.

The zoological source, together with new economic and ecological demands connected with energy saving and the "sustainability" of the environment, thus suggests new systems for the control of the various "environments" into which a
building can be broken down (lighting, heating, sound, atmosphere, tactile qualities) and, indirectly, the planning of new products, construction methods and
materials: for example, as thermal containers, buildings now require a "skin" or
membrane that, like the epidermis of an animal, is capable of providing a vari-
able response to the changing demands of the environment; the planning of the
architectural casing once again becomes more important than the traditional
planning of the installations with which it increasingly interacts.

8. Living forms

Both of these disciplinary settings move in accordance with a dominant functionalist conception of nature and the artificial works inspired by it, which rejects

or leaves on a secondary level the aesthetic problem of "living forms" in nature and in art – in other words, the apparent identity and the character inscribed in their material constitution.

In those same zoological sciences, this functionalist approach is so focused on activities clearly connected with the conservation of life that even the chromatic ornamentation of the epidermis – for example, the "accidental" appearance of silver crystals of guanine on the scales of fish or on the wings of butterflies – is seen only as a phenomenon conditioned by the metabolism.

But Adolf Portmann writes: "Living beings in relationship with the world are not just living machines whose activity is the metabolism in terms of which specifically they live. They are above all beings that manifest themselves in their peculiarity." "Animal interiority" and its "self-presentation" through the appearance of "good form," capable of imposing itself swiftly on the sight and other senses and of creating more intense impressions than other figures, are the primary characteristics of organisms in their relationship with the world; the principles of exchange, conservation, control of heat, reproduction and evolution are "subordinated" to them, as if to an essential biological fact. Thus, quoting Lorenz, "the bluethroat, the blackbird...give out the song that we find most beautiful, objectively the most complex, when they are almost relaxed, as if to create poetry for themselves. When the song becomes functional, as when the bird addresses a rival or seeks to arouse the attention of the female, all refinement is lost...the skilful imitations disappear completely, allowing the distinctive component inherent in their song to predominate, a strident sound that is quite certainly less beautiful."

The problem of form, i.e. substance, in architecture and industrial design objects seems to us to be precisely the same, on the level of analysis or design: that of finding a clear identity for things not as objects but as living subjects, or as "animated" configurations of matter, capable not only of permitting or promoting a function or a use but above all of expressing a meaning, a personal and social viewpoint about the human meaning of that very function, through the character that is materialized and made present in them.

9. Problems of the present

Now that all fear and friendship with the world of animals has been lost, left to the cognitive processes of children and the diversion of consumers considered as children (as in the duck-shaped drive-in on Long Island, noted by Peter Blake), a functionalist, technicized vision of nature and its economic exploitation have in recent decades become the new paradigm of meaning for the reality in which, more or less consciously and consentingly, we are immersed.

"The idea of the mastery of the world and of the producibility of what surrounds us is becoming increasingly prevalent," Portmann again writes forty years later, associating it "with the possibility that the most interesting forms of life may utterly vanish from the earth and that life itself may be represented (I am speaking of the more evident macroscopic forms) only by those organisms that we ourselves breed for purposes of practical utility or still tolerate for some other reason"; adding that "when we lose sight of these living testimonies of the greater processes of creation that we are allowed to witness, so much the more

does the awareness fade within us that in the final analysis our own creative activity also depends on those very forces, the unknown powers of the spirit." While animals passively gaze at us from a highly technological food chain – from genetic enclosures for experimental cloning, in conditions adverse to their original instincts, giving us new possibilities for survival – according to Umberto Galimberti, human beings will themselves "appear increasingly as passive executors of technical possibilities." As "emotional illiterates" we will witness the proliferation of arms and wars, and the destruction of the ecological system. Wealth and poverty will no longer be decided by our effective labor, and possibilities for total communication will become greater than the effective content that is to be communicated. On the other hand, as man disposes constitutionally of a "plasticity in adaptation" and culturally attains the stability that the animal possesses by instinct, a greater appropriateness in our feelings may raise us "to the level of generalized technical operation, making us emerge from the individual irresponsibility that enables the totalitarianism of technology to proceed undisturbed."
Let us hope that in this augured process of cognitive enlightenment for the present and possible futures of humanity – which also (and perhaps above all) lies in the hands of artists – animals will at least be respected.

Bibliographic references

L. B. Alberti, *L'architettura*, Il Polifilo, Milan 1989.

M. L. Cannarozzo, "'Macchina' e 'Organismo': la machine rationnelle di Le Corbusier," in V. Ugo (ed.), *Kritéria. Critica del discorso architettonico*, Guerini, Milan 1994.

D. Formaggio, *Arte*, Isedi, Milan 1973.

C. De Carli, "La velocità, nuovo 'tempo musicale' dell'Architettura," in *Stile*, no. 32–34, August–October 1943; and, by the same author, "Continuità," in *Domus*, no. 194, February 1944.

U. Galimberti, *Psiche e techne. L'uomo nell'età della tecnica*, Feltrinelli, Milan 1999.

G. Ottolini, *Forma e significato in architettura*, Laterza, Rome–Bari 1996.

A. Portmann, *Le forme viventi. Nuove prospettive della biologia*, Adelphi, Milan 1969.

Hic sunt leones.
When objects have the shapes and names of animals

Silvana Annicchiarico
*Curator of the Permanent Collection
of Italian Design of the Triennale di Milano*

Michel Foucault's *The Order of Things* begins, as is well known, by recalling a text by Borges, who, in turn referring to a "certain Chinese encyclopedia," proposes a unique and bizarre zoological classification, according to which "animals are divided into: (a) belonging to the Emperor, (b) embalmed, (c) tame, (d) suckling pigs, (e) sirens, (f) fabulous, (g) stray dogs, (h) included in the present classification, (i) frenzied, (j) innumerable, (k) drawn with a very fine camelhair brush, (l) *et cetera*, (m) having just broken the water pitcher, (n) that from a long way off look like flies"[1]. With its apparent paradoxicalness, this "atlas of the impossible," derisively placing heteroclite descriptions alongside the sequence of the letters of our alphabet, reminds us of the arbitrariness of any taxonomy or, if we prefer, the more or less codified subjectivity of any classification.

What seems impossible in Borges' catalogue, Foucault comments, is not "the propinquity of the things listed, but the very site on which their propinquity would be possible"[2]. Where indeed could "frenzied animals" and those designated simply as "innumerable" ever meet, except "in the immaterial sound of the voice pronouncing their enumeration," which is to say "in the non-place of language?"[3]. In other words: any classification, any taxonomy, is governed by an order made up of resemblances and differences intrinsic in the things ordered and classified, but one that, at the same time, does not exist "except in the grid created by a glance, an examination, a language"[4]. This was also recalled by Italo Calvino in his "Collezione di sabbia": "The secret fascination of a collection lies in what it reveals and what it hides of the secret impulse that led to its creation"[5]. As if to say: there must always be the "impulse" of a classifier in order to establish an order, a collection or a classification. There is no *objective* order unless it is legitimized by the *subjective* eye of the one who establishes it and institutes it as such.

What order, then, is to be found in the objects included in the exhibition *Animal House*, the second event in a series bearing the title – specifically as a tribute to Foucault – *The Order of Things*? What kind of view has instituted resemblances and differences in the heterogeneous array of Italian design objects so as to obtain the possible taxonomy that has guided the selection and combination of the objects exhibited?

At the very outset, as always, there is a question that entails an exploration: why do so many Italian design objects (over 200, according to the preliminary list drawn up and included as an appendix in this book) not only present a zoomorphic appearance but also often allude – even if only with the name given to them by the designer or manufacturer – to the animal world? With respect to the exhibition *Non sono una Signora* (I'm No Lady), which presented design objects linked by the fact that they all have women's names, the zoomorphic objects in *Animal House* are characterized by a more intrinsic and even more *necessary* relationship between signifier and signified. Erberto Carboni's *Delfino* (Dolphin) armchair alludes to the silhouette of a cetacean, Franco Albini's *Cicognino* (Little Stork) table suggests the profile of a stork, Marco Zanuso's *Grillo* (Cricket) telephone has an onomatopoeic ring that recalls the typical chirping of the insect from which it takes its name. Between words and things, therefore, there is in this case a relationship of greater contiguity, sometimes also of resemblance and analogy, or even – sometimes – of reciprocal implication: the object has *that* name because it *resembles* the animal commonly called by *that* very name. Or else, on the other hand, because the name helps to grasp the formal archetype inscribed in the appearance of the object, not always immediately evident to the distracted, superficial gaze of the observer. Thus the name reveals the designer's source of inspiration, disclosing the figurative plastic reference and offering a key for interpretation that goes beyond simple, immediate, utilitarian functionality and involves the object itself in a network of cultural allusions, echoes and suggestions. Forcing things a little, we might go so far as to say that the name predisposes the perceptual connection required to single out a new object (one *never seen before*), give it a specific identity and individuality, and insert it in a reasonably orderly manner into the collective cognitive wealth. It is somewhat like what happened to Marco Polo, in a celebrated example discussed by Umberto Eco. In Java, the author of *Il Milione* saw some animals that he had never seen before (rhinoceroses); he distinguished the body, the four legs and the horn, and as his culture and vocabulary placed at his disposal the notion of a unicorn as a quadruped with a horn on its head, he gave those unknown animals the designation of unicorns, although pointing out, with the insistence of an honest chronicler, the evident differences between the specific animals that he had just seen and the idea of a unicorn that was stored in his mind[6]. In some ways, something similar happens with Elio Martinelli's *Cobra* lamp: an object *never seen before* is registered in our mind not only by the reference to the idea of a lamp (which would be as reductive as classifying a rhinoceros simply as an animal) but also by the reference to another form that is *already known*, suggested by the name (specifically, that of the cobra), which enables us to distinguish that particular lamp (or rather, that *type* of lamp) from the "lighting menagerie" of all the other lamps that fill our homes and commercial showrooms.

We do not intend here to delve into the long-standing problem – which has to do with both philosophy and semiotics – concerning our perception of things and the question of whether it depends on the structure of our cognitive apparatus or on our linguistic apparatus. In the present context, what matters is rather to reason about the *symbolic economy* that certain nominalistic choices set into motion, about the kind of relationship that the name attributed to an object seeks of the person who has enjoyment of it, about the field of effect that a certain combination of an object's form and the name given to it ultimately radiates around it. As soon as we start to occupy ourselves with zoomorphic and zoonomous objects, we cannot fail to point out that in the epistemology of modernity the figure of the animal is charged with symbolic values, especially when it evokes the idea of *disappearance, absence* or *remoteness*. In classical culture and in pre-industrial society, in a condition of objective, everyday promiscuity, the figure of the animal either became merely a symbol of radical otherness ("*Hic sunt leones*"), or else it often lent itself to exemplarily educative, admonitory tales in the form of Aesop's fables ("*The fox and the grapes*"), or else again it cathartically sparked off the imagination through the myth of metamorphosis and the fantasy of the perpetual instability of form that it implied. In any case, nature was a "forest of symbols," and any bestiary offered allegories that were begging to be interpreted[7]. In contemporary culture, similar symbolic treatments of animality have certainly not disappeared, and indeed survive in various forms: one recalls, in a literary context, the use of the animal made by a writer who is sensitive to suggestions of the fantastic, such as Dino Buzzati[8], or of the original revival of the form of the fable undertaken by an author such as Alessandro Boffa, who uses animal behavior to describe the neuroses, oddities and vanities of human beings[9]. But in these cases, what is set in play is the archetypal structure of animality, its ontological substance, as it were, not its ability to tell us something specific and unique about our present. In order to find cases of animals used in this sense, one must instead, almost inevitably, turn to examples that allude to *something that is disappearing*: one need only think of how Pier Paolo Pasolini saw in the disappearance of fireflies in summer nights an unmistakable symptom of the end of peasant culture[10], or of how the panda has almost become the logo of animality in need of protection and in danger of extinction, or again – in the realm of mass culture and popular entertainment – of the possibility of portending an absence assumed by a non-existent animal such as the *sarchiapone* in a famous television sketch by Walter Chiari and Carlo Campanini, studied in masterly fashion by Umberto Eco as an example of a "sealed box"[11]. In all these examples, the animal in question becomes the symbolic sign of something that *does not exist and never has existed* (the *sarchiapone*), or that *has existed but no longer exists* (the firefly), or that *still exists but is in danger of no longer existing soon* (the panda).

It is our hypothesis that, on a symbolic plane, zoomorphic and zoonomous design objects also express an analogous sign of extinction. That they portend an absence. That they indicate an expulsion and in some way help to make it bearable.

In their morphological and/or nominalistic obviousness, these objects – accepted into the domestic dimension of the *intérieur* – actually offer themselves as *surrogates* of the animality that does not (and cannot) have a place in the modern dwelling. In a way, they are affective prostheses: in the cultural space *par excellence* (that of architecture, of the home as a planned dwelling removed from the snares and threats and rigors of nature), they evoke the memory of lost, rejected naturalness and promiscuity. In short, they mark the recovery of repressed memories: they welcome animality back in the form of a designed object, after initially expelling it in its "beastly," uncontrollable naturalness. The process is well illustrated, with almost paradigmatic clarity, in Jean-Pierre Jeunet's film *Amélie* (2001), in which a red fish in a classic domestic "glass bowl" – lovingly looked after by the central character – cannot bear living in an "unnatural" environment such as that of a Paris flat, and so, with a bold flick of its tail, it leaps out of the water in the bowl, almost as if it wanted to commit suicide. Amélie returns the fish to its natural habitat (by throwing it into the river) and gradually replaces it with "artificial icons" of animality: first she photographs clouds shaped like a rabbit or a little bear, then she decorates her home with a picture of fish and with zoomorphic ornaments (for example, a piglet dressed as an English aristocrat, holding a lampshade as if it were a parasol). They are "fantasy animals" that act as a substitute for the fish that has been returned to nature, in a way preserving the impression and the trace that it has left behind. Setting metaphor aside, something analogous has been happening for some time in our real homes, either with all the anonymous, common objects that have now assumed stereotyped animal forms (the coin bank shaped like a plump piglet, the door draft stopper in the form of a caterpillar that clings perfectly to the floor, the porcelain container shaped like a little rabbit that is used for storing cotton balls on a women's dressing table), or with mass-produced objects of more experimental design. According to Ugo La Pietra, the "technomorphic bestiary" initially appeared particularly in the experiments of the graphic underground or so-called counter-design: "In the fifties, in London, a series of small publications appeared, with drawings by Hoffnung in which commonly used objects became animals and in which objects with some parts expediently integrated into musical instruments acquired new functions: an ironic game that continually shifted the attention from the world of objects to that of animals in an exercise of imaginative exploration, inventing a bestiary in which commonly used objects were the central figures. The sixties were distinguished by Jean Solé's *Les animaleries*, in which the back of a chair became a kangaroo or a bird's beak became a compass"[12]. Soon afterwards, starting in the late sixties, objects themselves were assailed by flows of zoomorphic contamination, as one can gather from, *inter alia*, the catalogue of innovative objects singled out by Andrea Branzi, where the fact that they all have animal names is no accident: "Theoretical products with a similar metaphorical content in those years were the linear and theoretically endless seating units designed by Marco Zanuso (*Lombrico* [Worm] in 1967 for C&B) and by Cini Boeri (*Serpentone* [Big Snake], made of connectable polyurethane disks for Arflex in 1971), Bellini's *Camaleonda* random seating system for C&B in 1970–71 and the *Boalum* spiral tube lamp by Livio Castiglioni and Gianfranco Frattini for Artemide in 1970: all radical designs that simulated the end of the individual object within a system of uninterrupted mass production"[13]. It was also Branzi, in the eighties, who gave the name *Animali domestici* (Pets) to a series of items of furniture and clothing designed to give a new look to the domestic setting. "As hybrids of archetypal materials and anonymous industrial goods, a combination of Arte

Povera and precision design, they lend their very own expression to the search for possible ways to combine technical feasibility and respect for nature"[14]. The name attributed to the series was far from gratuitous: like real, live pets, the objects designed by Branzi aspired to be perceived as living creatures "that come from a strange but kindred world"[15].

Since then, perhaps in harmony with the increasing sensitivity to ecology and nature, the zoophilous trend in design has been strengthened and consolidated in an increasingly conspicuous manner. On an international level, after Bernard Rancillac's historic *Elephant* seat in 1966 and Eero Aarnio's *Pony* seat in 1970, one need only think of the lamps by the Finnish designer Stefan Lindfors: *Lagostinux* looks like an insect – maybe a wasp, or perhaps a queen bee – that hovers in the air with its red wings as if fluttering on a shifting beam of light, whereas the lighting equipment that Lindfors designed for the Helsinki airport calls to mind huge, steel dragonflies that have arrogantly emerged from the designer's unconscious. On a national level, also, almost all the most important Italian designers have produced zoomorphic or zoonomous objects, and not accidentally: from Munari (the little monkey *Zizi*) to Castiglioni (the *Gatto* [Cat] lamp), from Gae Aulenti (the *Pipistrello* [Bat] lamp) to Anna Castelli Ferrieri (the *Piggy* ottoman). Not to mention, in more recent times, the zoomorphic furniture designed by Ico Parisi for Lietti in 1992. Sometimes, but rarely, they are domestic animals. Sometimes, and more frequently, the names or shapes of design objects evoke exotic, fierce, wild, predatory animals (Elio Martinelli's *Serpente* [Snake] lamp, Paolo Tilche's *Giraffa* [Giraffe] bookcase, Ico Parisi's

Rinoceronte [Rhinoceros] chest of drawers, Giugiaro's prototype for the *Orca* [Killer Whale] car). Sometimes, also, it is the advertising that associates the object with a particular animal: for example, in a famous Alessi campaign, there was a picture of a cat crouching behind Michael Graves's kettle with a bird, or there was the Poltrona Frau 2001 advertising campaign by Armando Testa, in which "It so happened that a bull, provoked by the fiery red of *Vanity Fair*, was tamed by the legendary quality of its beauty. Or that a chameleon, seduced by the dazzling colors of *Eos*, tried to imitate them all. Or that a wolf, deceived by the unique forms of *Dafne* (Daphne), began to howl"[16].

The home is animated by these metaphorical presences like a virtual zoo, and the reincarnation of animality flourishes again within the *ratio* of modern and technological design.

As if they have emerged from some kind of "Noah's ark," these zoomorphic objects extend the confines of the home, stretching or prolonging them to the realm of nature: perhaps out of nostalgia for lost instincts and strayed forms, or to give the "civilized" user simulacra and icons that help him – in their way – to recall that he too forms part of the great zoological atlas of the world. If it is true, as Walter Benjamin wrote, that "dwelling means leaving traces"[17], these objects conserve and preserve important marks and traces that tell us something, not without importance, about our relationship with things, and also more generally about our way of perceiving, using, cataloguing and, ultimately, reconnecting them with the world.

Certainly there is often a distinctly ironic quality in the animal form that appears behind the morphology of a lamp or a seat. Frequently one senses a playful or humorous aim in the designer, sometimes nostalgic and sometimes sarcastic, as if in certain allusive forms the designer recognizes a kind of transfer, or the impossibility of existing without a body. This does not happen only with animals: every chair has "legs," almost all armchairs have "arms" and a "back." The body deposits itself in objects, gives its name to their parts and ergonomically inspires their structure. Zoomorphic objects, however, offer the human body a contiguity with different corporeal models.

It is a little like what happens with certain idiomatic phrases in colloquial language. "You're an ass!" people say. Or, "That man is a lion..." The language metaphorically assumes an identity that is held to be universally known (here, that of the ass or lion) in order to denote and express – swiftly, almost by a cognitive short circuit – the identity, character and physical appearance of an individual. One sometimes has the impression that something similar happens with certain objects: I call a seat *Canguro* (Kangaroo) or a lamp *Papero* (Gosling) either to make clear, quickly, what model has inspired me, or else because I am surprised by a resemblance that unexpectedly "pricks me" as I am observing the form of an object that I have produced or designed. Associations of ideas. An intoxication (and irony) of similarity. The pleasure (and play) of analogy. This is how the names of objects originate: with linguistic acrobatics and stunts that clarify modes and forms of design.

An entomologist of design could classify the objects selected and presented in this exhibition in various ways. He could adopt a descriptive, functionalist taxonomy, distinguishing, for example, between objects that conserve an animal trace only in name, those that have a zoomorphic reminder only in form, and those that appear zoophilous both in form and name. Or else he could hypothesize a subdivision between objects that evoke domestic animals and those that instead refer to a more remote, exotic animality, playing on the oxymoron inherent in the act of interjecting otherness into the domestic (and domesticated) setting of the *intérieur*. Or, yet again, he could invent an impossible taxonomy *à la* Borges, unleashing the imagination in the creation of the most bizarre, unhomogeneous, surprising categories possible.

The exhibition *Animal House* instead adopts other criteria and proposes a different classification. The objects selected have been subdivided into four categories, based more on the nature and species of the animals evoked by the objects than on particular, specific characteristics of the objects themselves. So there are objects that evoke *aquatic animals* (*Medusa, Folpo, Moscardino, Delfino*), *flying animals* (*Vespa, Pipistrello, Heron, Bird*), *terrestrial animals* (*Topolino, Grillo, Gatto, Tartaruga*) and *animals of play and fantasy* (*Fritz, Moby Dick, Snoopy, Zizì*). The risk inherent in the decision to place within the same "class" (specifically, that of *flying* or of *aquatic* animals) objects belonging to different typologies and having very different characteristics of design and function is counterbalanced and recompensed by the advantage of being able to hypothesize new groupings capable of illustrating scenarios that are new by comparison with those offered by the established utilitarian value. If a seat (*Papillon* [Butterfly]), a lamp (*Falena* [Moth]) and a side table (*Cicognino* [Little

Stork]) all refer – despite the radical diversity of the act of design that created them – to an "animal that flies," this means that there is something profound – albeit not immediately tangible – that they have in common: perhaps lightness, perhaps a certain plastic/dynamic impulse towards an upward movement, or perhaps an ambition to assume, in their own form, the light, sober elegance of an animal capable of detaching itself from the ground. Similarly, the objects that refer to animals of play or fantasy effect a kind of metalinguistic restructuring, transferring to the world of mass-production – sometimes playfully, sometimes lyrically – the mythopoeic power that emanates from the non-existent animals (*Moby Dick, Calimero, Snoopy*) from which they derive their own identity. Such a classification also has the advantage of demonstrating unmistakably how each kind of habitat has been considered in the process of the renaming of objects, to the extent of configuring the domestic space assigned to accommodating zoonomous and zoomorphous objects as a kind of symbolic microcosmos in which the macrocosm of nature continually deposits manifestations of itself.

In a famous passage, Walter Benjamin reminds us that "forms [are] the true mystery of nature," that "in the final analysis all the great conquests in the sphere of forms take place as the result of technical discoveries," and that "only now are we beginning to sense what forms lie hidden within machines"[18]. In order to make his idea more clear, Benjamin quotes an extract from Marx that recalls a prototype of the locomotive "with two feet" raised alternately, "like a horse." The development of technology and mechanics would seem subsequently to have emancipated the locomotive-machine from the corporeal form that had originally inspired it (the legs of a horse), conferring an abstract form (that of wheels) unmindful of the bodily function (the ability to generate movement) that the machine sought to replace and improve. Something similar has also happened with design objects on some occasions: thanks to the development of the technique and capability of design, objects have progressively absorbed and concealed the form of the body – human or animal – that inspired them and that they aimed to replace. But with objects such as those that are included in this exhibition, we are dealing, in a way, with an inversion of the trend: the object returns to the body, removing the technical mask and confessing its true origin. On some occasions, the operation inscribed within the zoophilous objects catalogued here is one of revelation and return. Not an act of nostalgia but a gesture of disclosure: almost an invitation to the object (and the person who enjoys it) to accept awareness of itself and its own history.

Notes

1. Michel Foucault, *Les mots et les choses*, Gallimard, Paris 1966 (English trans. *The Order of Things*, Vintage Books, New York 1994, p. xv).
2. *Ibid.*, p. xvi.
3. *Ibid.*, p. xvi f.
4. *Ibid.*, p. xx.
5. Italo Calvino, "Collezione di sabbia," in *Corriere della Sera*, 25 June 1974; now in *Collezione di sabbia*, Mondadori, Milan 1994, p. 7.
6. Umberto Eco, *Kant e l'ornitorinco*, Bompiani, Milan 1997, p. 43 ff. (English trans. *Kant and the Platypus*, Secker & Warburg, London 1999).
7. Mirella Levi D'Ancona, *Lo zoo del Rinascimento. Il significato degli animali nella pittura italiana dal XIV al XVI secolo*, Fazzi Editore, Lucca 2001; Francesco Mezzalira, *Bestie e bestiari. La rappresentazione degli animali dalla preistoria al Rinascimento*, Allemandi Editore, Turin 2001; Paolo Pettinari, *Bestie, uomini, virtù. Esempi da due bestiari medioevali*, in "L'Area di Broca," XXI, 59, 1994.
8. Dino Buzzati, *Bestiario*, Mondadori, Milan 1991.
9. Alessandro Boffa, *Sei una bestia, Viskovitz!*, Garzanti, Milan 1998.
10. Pier Paolo Pasolini, "Il vuoto del potere in Italia," in *Corriere della Sera*, 1 February 1975, now in *Scritti corsari*, Garzanti, Milan 1990, p. 128.
11. Umberto Eco, *Kant e l'ornitorinco, op. cit.*, p. 251 ff.
12. Ugo La Pietra, "Bestiario tecnomorfo," *Modo*, no. 28, April 1980, p. 67.
13. Andrea Branzi, *Il design italiano 1964–1990*, Electa, Milan 1996, p. 59.
14. "Animali domestici," in *100 Masterpieces from the Vitra Design Museum Collection*, Vitra Design Museum, Weil am Rhein 1996, p. 232.
15. *Ibid.*
16. From the foreword to the catalogue of the Poltrona Frau 2001 advertising campaign.
17. Walter Benjamin, *Parigi capitale del XIX secolo*, Einaudi, Turin 1986, p. 13.
18. *Ibid.*, p. 213.

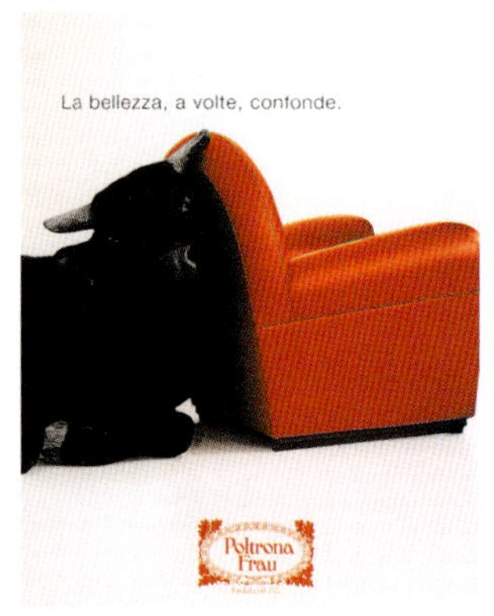

Vanity Fair. Frau Archive.
Advertising Campaign 2001,
Armando Testa

Terrestrial animals

Some jump (the cricket and the kangaroo), others crawl (the worm, the cobra and the boa), and others scurry (the mouse). The terrestrial animals associated with the objects included in this section have various ways of moving on the ground, but they all rest their legs or body on the earth. The objects that take their names from these animals also attach special importance to the relationship with the ground: sometimes they stand on it, sometimes they lie on it, and sometimes – as in the case of the Fiat *Topolino* (Little Mouse) – they glide over it. There is almost always a formal relationship between the object and the animal from which it takes its name, sometimes in the form of a synecdoche: the headlights of the *Topolino* recall the ears of a mouse; the body of the *Tartaruga* cable telephony receiver is reminiscent of the shell of a tortoise; the profile of seating units such as *Piggy* or *Pecorelle* are inspired by the morphologies of pigs or sheep. *Lombrico* recalls the segmented linearity of a worm, whereas *Cobra*, *Hebi* and *Boalum* mimic attitudes and postures typical of reptiles. In short, nature's zoo has left its imprint on the world of design objects. Or, if you prefer, the culture of design has rediscovered its archetypes and formal origins in the great animal encyclopedia of the world.

Topolino 500

Automobile
Dante Giacosa
1936
Fiat

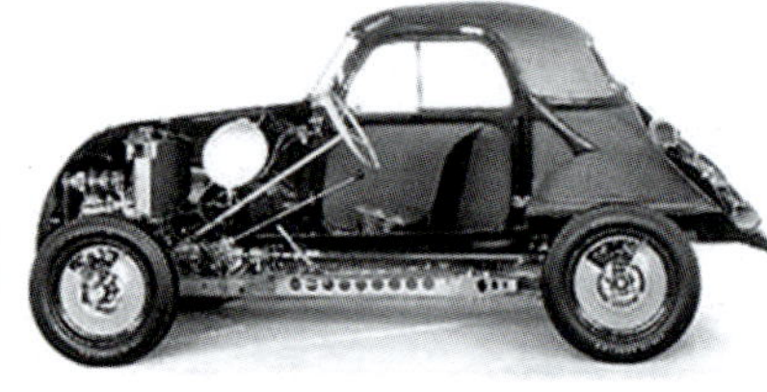

Launched onto the market on June 15, 1936, the popular Fiat 500 was immediately given the name of *Topolino* (Little Mouse) by public demand, because of the two headlamps on the wings that made it look like a little mouse. Capable of doing 100 km on 5 liters of petrol at a maximum speed of 85 kph, this low-cost car has a small interior that can accommodate two adults, with a space at the rear suitable for children or baggage. Initially available at a price of 8,900 lire (10 times the salary of a bank clerk), it led to a spectacular increase in annual vehicle registrations, putting Fiat in a competitive position in the European market, with over 7% of total car sales.
In 1955 it disappeared from the Fiat price-list, replaced by the 600. It is estimated that over 500,000 *Topolino* cars were produced in less than twenty years.

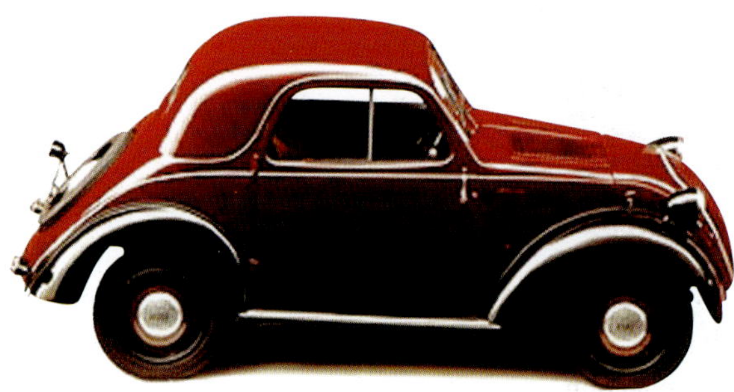

Pietro Pedrini Collection

Lombrico

Divan
Marco Zanuso
1967
C&B

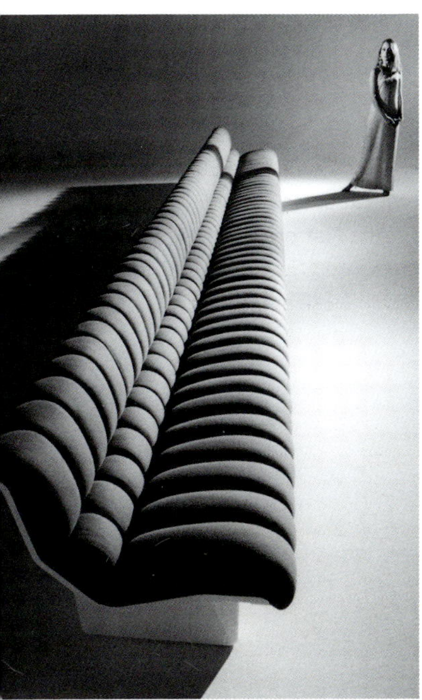

B&B Collection

Based on the principles of modularity and connectivity, with a 20-cm modular ring theoretically capable of being repeated indefinitely, Marco Zanuso's *Lombrico* (Worm) was presented experimentally at the Triennale in 1968, but it never went into production. The designer's idea was to achieve "a development in seating that would go beyond the home and take upholstery across the boundary into the public space of institutions" (Manolo De Giorgi, *Marco Zanuso architetto*, Skira, Milan 1999, p. 116). Typologically, however, the idea was too innovative to be accepted by the marketplace. *Lombrico* remains a prototype: free of preconceptions, courageous and, in its way, utopian. It was the result of modernist impulses of the sixties, but also of demands to streamline production for the sake of flexibility. The name given to it is cleverly suggestive, encompassing its linear workings and curved, segmented structure with masterful irony: like a huge, extendable worm clinging perfectly to the ground.

Tartaruga

Cable telephony receiver
Roberto Menghi
1957
SIT Siemens

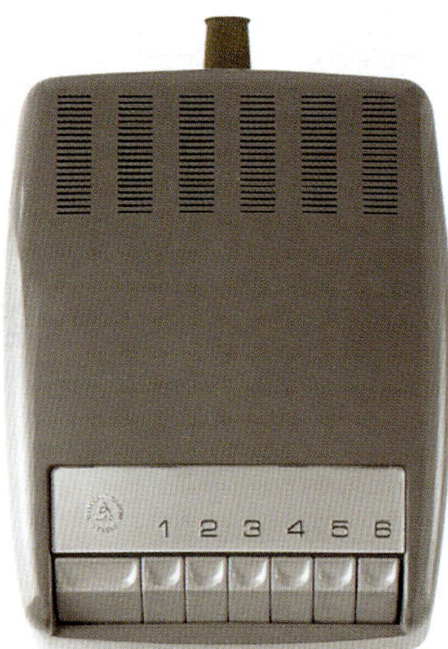

In the fifties, the processes of adjustment and technological innovation within the media led to the success of *cable telephony*: a new way of transmitting radio programs by telephone cable. The receiver was an automatic program selector that acted as a bridge between the normal telephone network and private radio sets. Roberto Menghi designed for Siemens a receiver with an understated casing. The name *Tartaruga* (Tortoise) has an ironic connotation that is both analogous and antithetical: the apparatus bears the outer shell of an animal that symbolizes slowness, but it aspired to be a symbol of new technological speed in the transmission of data, signals and information.

Triennale di Milano Collection

Gatto

Lamp
Achille Castiglioni – Pier Giacomo Castiglioni
1962
Flos

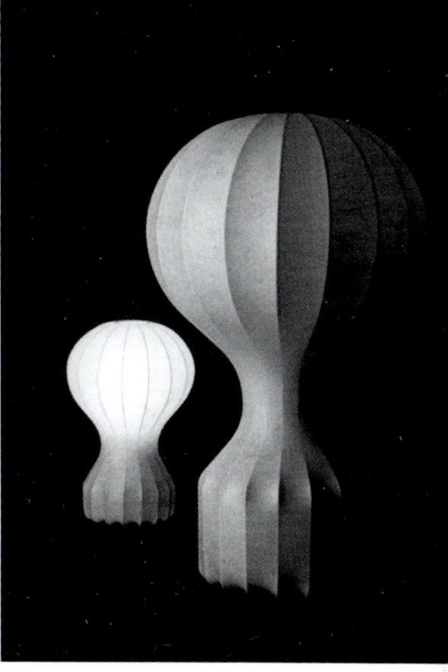

With *Gatto* (Cat) and *Gatto Piccolo* (Little Cat) the Castiglioni brothers continued their investigation – begun in 1960 – of the expressive capacity of a synthetic fiber known as "cocoon," already used in the early fifties by George Nelson and Isamu Noguchi. The *Gatto* lamps followed the *Viscontea* and *Taraxacum* lamps (1960) – in which the skeleton consisted of a thin white metal rod on which a film of plastic polymer was sprayed, acquiring its shape when the structure was rotated – and the *Fantasma* (Phantom) lamp (1961) by Afra and Tobia Scarpa, made with the same fiber. Conceived as a single block with an illuminated upper spherical section, the *Gatto* lamps are an ironic, playful interpretation of the table lamp typology.
The name and shape refer to a cat in the act of arching its back, or curling itself up like a kind of ribbed ball.

Flos Collection

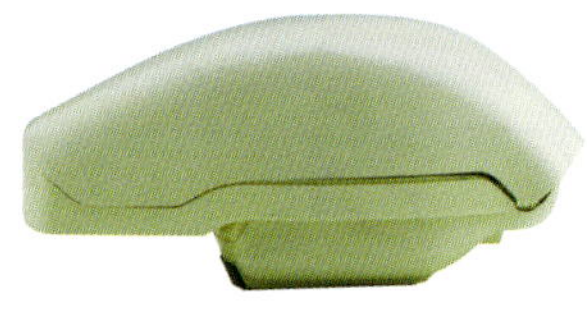

Grillo

Telephone
Marco Zanuso
Richard Sapper
1967
SIT Siemens

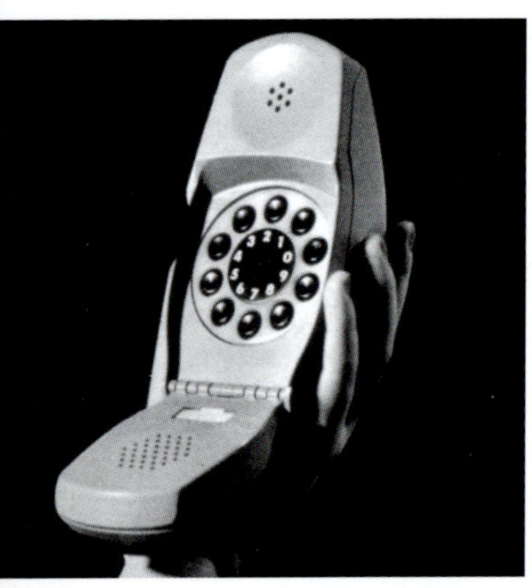

Triennale di Milano Collection

Like a small animal contracted and closed in upon itself, *Grillo* (Cricket) has a carapace-like back that conceals its points of contact with the "outside" world. When opened, one can dial a number and begin a conversation; the closing of the apparatus, on the other hand, coincides with the interruption of communication. The opening and closing are effected by means of hinges that connect the two parts of the device. A long cable extends like a tail from the carapace-back, permitting greater mobility. Small, compact and uncomplicated, *Grillo* is a forerunner of the new typology of mobile, cordless and cellular phones: the device is not divided into separate parts (base and handset), but forms a single unit. The ringing mechanism, however, is transferred to a wall fixture with three holes that make a unique trilling sound from which the object's name is partly derived. Marco Zanuso describes it thus: "...the general briefing was clear – eliminate the fixed quality and enhance mobility, barely attaching it by a length of cable that nevertheless kept the telephone connected to the socket... The object's name, *Grillo*, was partly influenced by physiognomic aspects, vaguely suggesting the shape of a cricket, especially the back... The new, informal, private posture that the object suggested to the user gave the design a *je ne sais quoi* with a personal, intimate, secret, whispering quality that was almost sexy" (Marco Zanuso, in *Stile industria*, ADI, no. 3, September 1995, pp. 48–50).

Cobra

Lamp
Elio Martinelli
1968
Martinelli Luce

Martinelli Luce Collection

In the sixties, Martinelli defined itself as a company that concentrated particularly on making overtly zoomorphic lamps: after Gae Aulenti's *Pipistrello* (Bat, 1965), other notable examples included *Serpente* (Serpent, 1965), *Le Rondini* (The Swallows, 1984), *Gabbiano* (Seagull, 1992) and *Le Formiche* (The Ants, 1994), all designed by Elio Martinelli. *Cobra* is undoubtedly one of the most interesting models in the series. The swiveling resin arm that connects the base to the reflector enables the lamp to adopt two of the typical positions of the reptile from which it takes its name: when the reflector is positioned above the base, the object has the profile of a cobra with head erect and ready to strike, whereas when the reflector is reversed, the lamp has the silhouette of a snake sinuously gliding forward with its head extended.

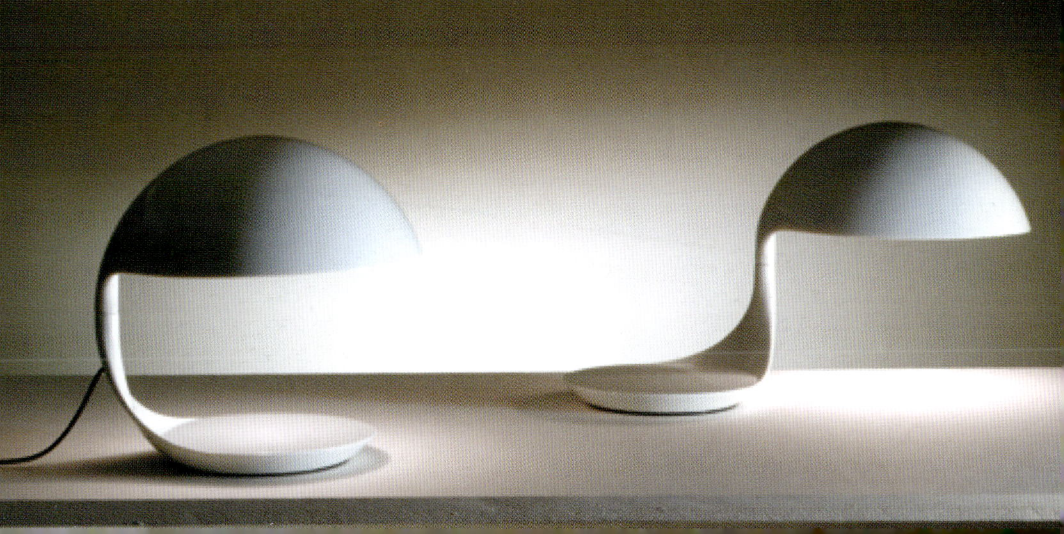

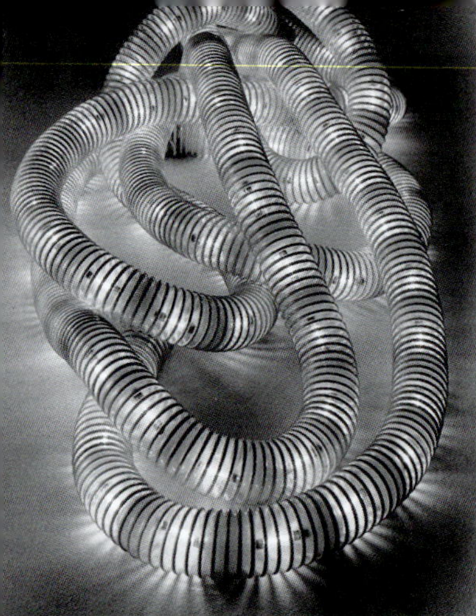

Boalum

Lamp
Livio Castiglioni
Gianfranco Frattini
1969
Artemide

As the name suggests, *boa-lum* is a kind of illuminated snake: a tube of flexible, transparent resin, two meters long (but modular so that theoretically it can achieve an infinite length), containing twenty special cylindrical bulbs held in place by rings and a metal spiral that carries an electrical current. It can be placed in any part of a room and is designed to diffuse a soft, non-directional light. In line with the principles of modernity, flexibility and transformability expressed in the late sixties, *Boalum* can be hung, coiled, stretched out or tangled up. The idea came to designers Livio Castiglioni and Gianfranco Frattini when they were in a garden beside a swimming-pool, watching a pool cleaner in operation: fascinated by the movement of the tube, they tried to imagine an object that would have the same lightness and simplicity, but could at the same time function as an unusual source of light.

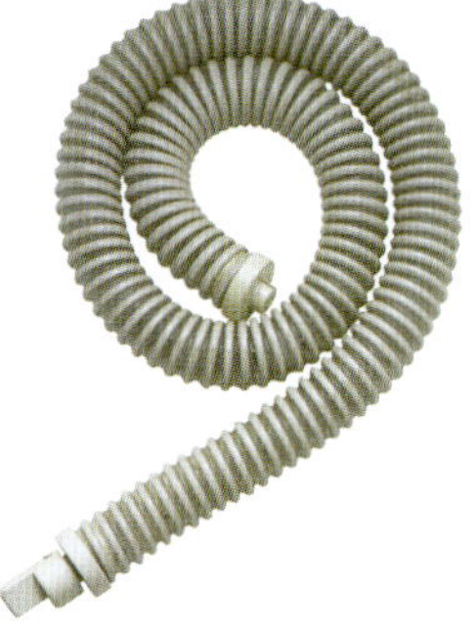

Primate

Seat
Achille Castiglioni
Pier Giacomo Castiglioni
1970
Zanotta

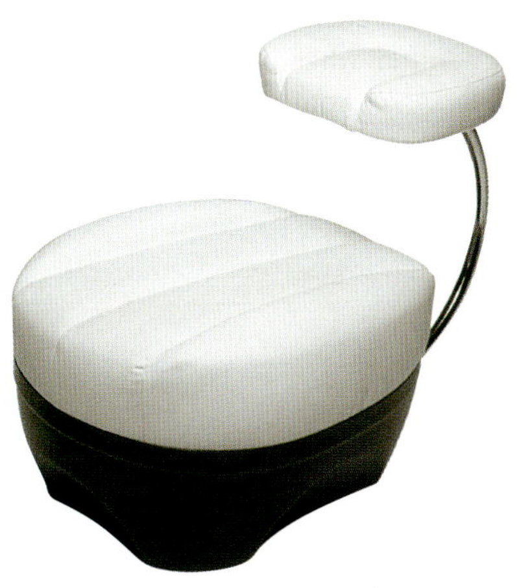

Zanotta Collection

In order to sit with the body erect one must kneel. *Primate* is imbued with this paradox: it is like a prie-dieu with a seat connected by a steel shaft to a polystyrene base filled with polyurethane. The posture assumed by the person using it is reminiscent of the attitude of a primate attempting to stand erect. In an interview in 1988, Achille Castiglioni explained: "The idea of this kind of seat came to me when I was thinking of small children, who often cannot reach the level of the table when they are sitting on a chair, and so they kneel on the chair and put a cushion between their legs and the seat, and that's the position in which they do their homework. I used to do the same... In oriental countries, however, this position is adopted by people sitting in groups, and it is considered a very dignified posture and not at all unseemly..."

Primate was presented in the exhibition *Italian Furniture* in Tokyo in 1984, as one of several items – all created by Castiglioni – that contributed to the presentation of a "polycentric" table as a new expression of conviviality, continuing the exploratory work he carried out earlier in Villa Olmo in 1957, and in Florence in 1965.

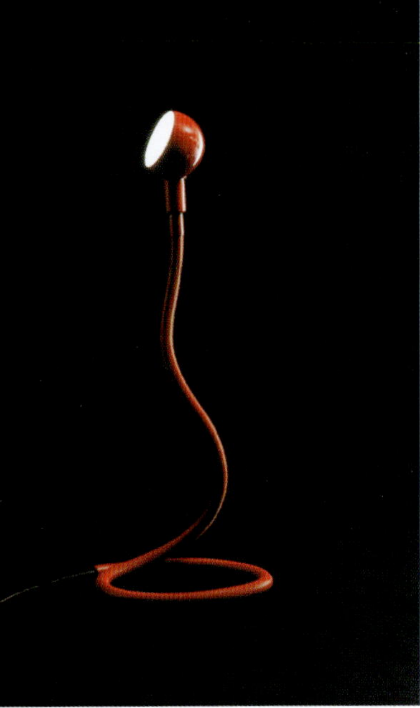

Hebi

Lamp
Isao Hosoe
1970
Valenti

Triennale di Milano Collection

Flexible and sinuous, constructed almost entirely out of items already existing in the marketplace – such as the PVC tubing generally used to sheathe cables in walls – *Hebi* is a typical example of do-it-yourself design.

The designer, Isao Hosoe, says so openly: "According to Lévi-Strauss, a do-it-yourself enthusiast is someone with a bag who goes off to the forest and picks up and collects things that are there, and then he empties out the bag and finds the things he has collected and gives them a new order. That's how it was for *Hebi*: I started off with the flexible tube, and among the various elements and components available I found a suitable object for the head of the lamp. I didn't manage to find the right base, but perhaps, unconsciously, I didn't want to find it.

Then I tried twisting the flexible tube, and the lamp appeared... Hence the name *Hebi*, which means snake in Japanese."

Thanks to the bendable quality of the flexible tube, the lamp can assume postures similar to those of a snake aroused by the hypnotic sounds of a storybook snake charmer.

Canguro

Chair
Giorgina Castiglioni
Giorgio Gaviraghi
1970
Gufram

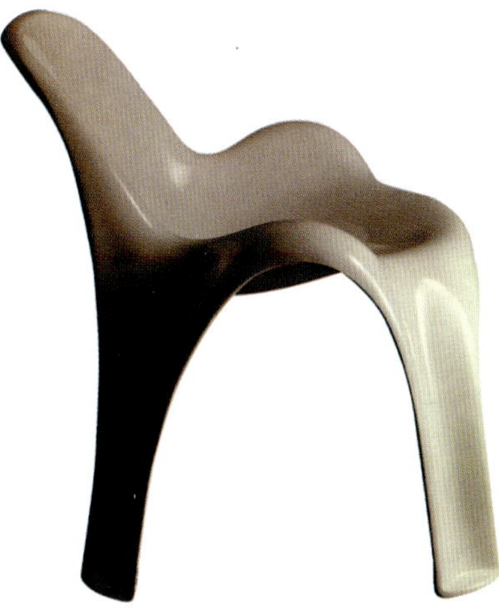

Triennale di Milano Collection

During the transition from the sixties to the seventies, one of the typical themes of Italian design was *stackability*: among those who tested their mettle with it were Vico Magistretti (with *Selene* in 1964 and *Vicario* in 1970–71), Joe Colombo (who experimented with his *4860-61/5* model for Kartell in 1968) and Alberto Rosselli (with the *P110* for Saporiti in 1971). As Andrea Branzi has noted, this theme represented a myth rather than a serviceable feature, embodying the dream "of a mass-produced reality invading the world" (Andrea Branzi, *Il design italiano 1964–1990*, Electa, Milan 1996, p. 59). Nevertheless, stackable seating became one of the trends of design practice from that period.

Giorgina Castiglioni's *Canguro* (Kangaroo) embodies that exploration: made from reinforced polyester, it combines the functional requirement of stackability with a zoophilic reference to an exotic animal, the kangaroo, which seems to be indicated by (or may have been the origin of) the upward thrust of the legs (designed as if they were on the verge of leaping) and the "marsupial" pouch that occupies the traditional position of the seat.

Pecorelle

Seat
Cini Boeri
Laura Griziotti
1979
Arflex

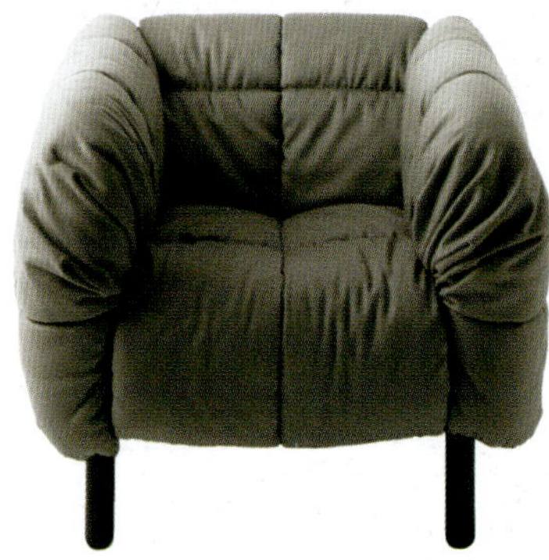

In 1972, with the collaboration of Laura Griziotti, Cini Boeri designed the first *Strips*, a large family of furniture for relaxation (armchairs, settees and beds) that developed over the subsequent years and gave rise to a remarkable variety of models.

Made of foam polyurethane expanded to various densities and upholstered with a covering of polyester fiber, the *Strips* presented new models of comfort within a design focus always very intent on emphasizing the notion of the human dwelling.

The *Pecorelle* (Little Sheep) model, 1979, belongs to the *Strips* series, although the addition of legs represents a variation: seen in profile it has a vaguely ovine shape that recalls the typical silhouette of a sheep. The zoomorphic reference included in the name also highlights some of the object's intrinsic qualities: softness, a feeling of warmth, and an invitation to rest and relax. Just as sheep cluster together in flocks, these pieces of furniture can be placed together and arranged in different combinations.

Triennale di Milano Collection

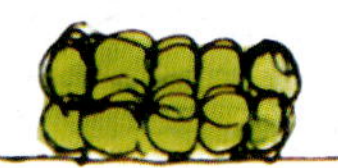
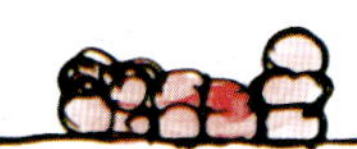
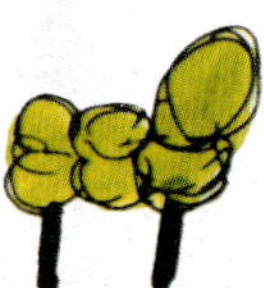

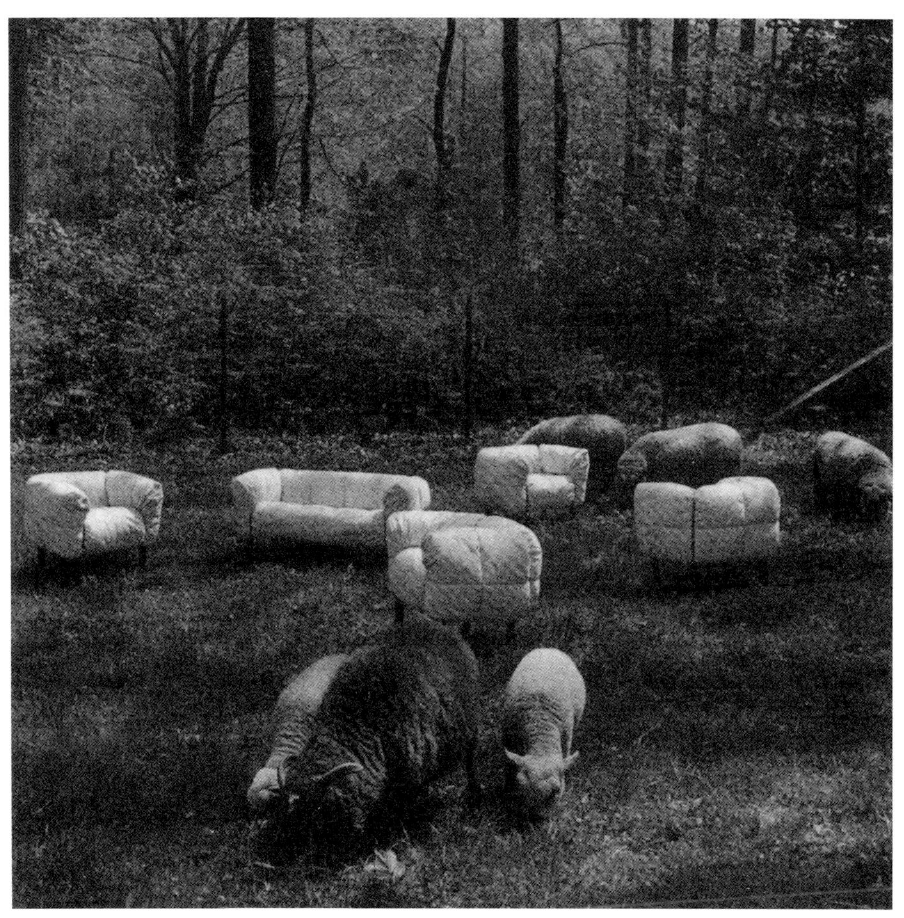

Piggy

Ottoman
Anna Castelli Ferrieri
1991
Matteograssi

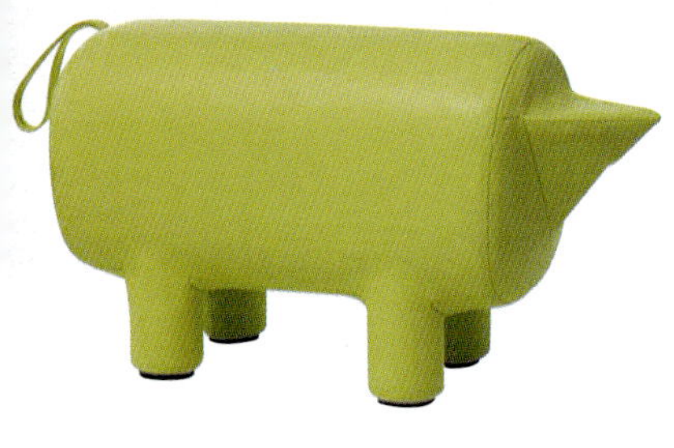

Matteograssi Collection

"In London, a few decades ago at Liberty's, there were objects shaped like animals and covered with leather which I bought for my children. They were extraordinary objects: you could sit on them, pull their tail, their nose, their eyes... Then they disappeared. *Piggy* comes from them." That is how Anna Castelli Ferrieri describes the origin of this upholstered leather seat: four little "legs," a tail, a snout on which you can place an ashtray or a glass, and a multipurpose seat suitable for straddling, sitting on in a proper fashion or using to prop up one's feet. The name and shape have an appealingly domestic, familiar, playful quality, recalling morphologies remembered from childhood.

In 1997, on the occasion of the major exhibition devoted to this designer in Chicago, curator Claudia Donà exhibited various *Piggy* ottomans in different colors against a background of vertical furniture also made by Ferrieri, as a tribute to the book just published by Marco D'Eramo, *Il maiale e il grattacielo. Chicago: una storia del nostro futuro* (The Pig and the Skyscraper).

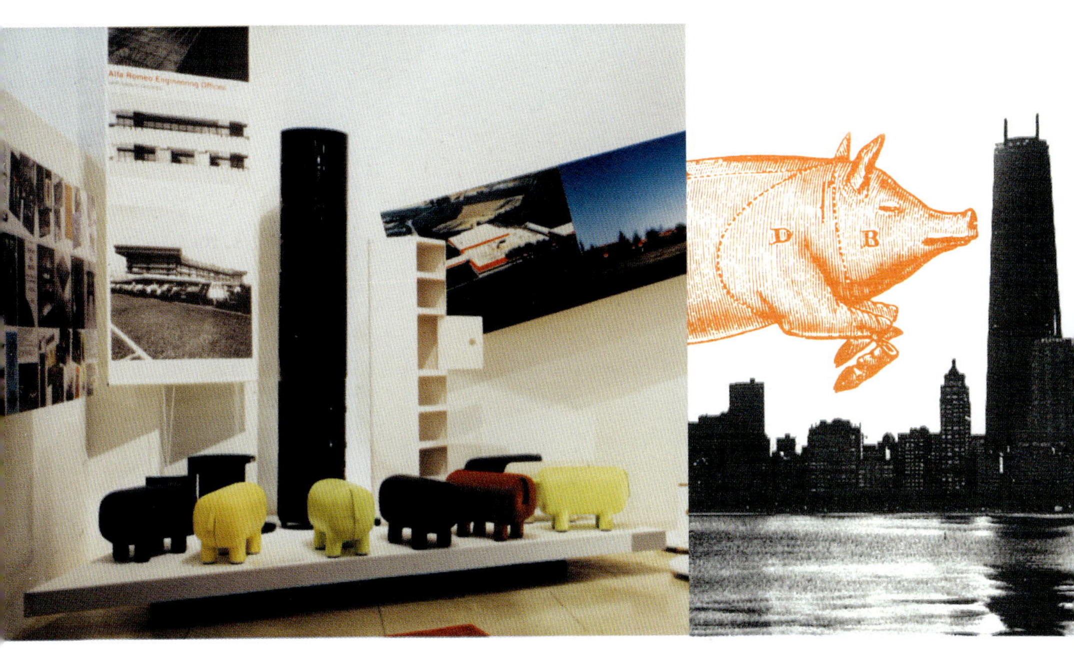

In *Piggy* one can also find the tension, rigor and creativity characteristic of all Ferrieri's work. As reported by Claudia Donà, Ferrieri herself has said: "As I go on my way, I am aware of the responsibility that I take upon myself every time that I add a new presence to a physical world that is already overpopulated."

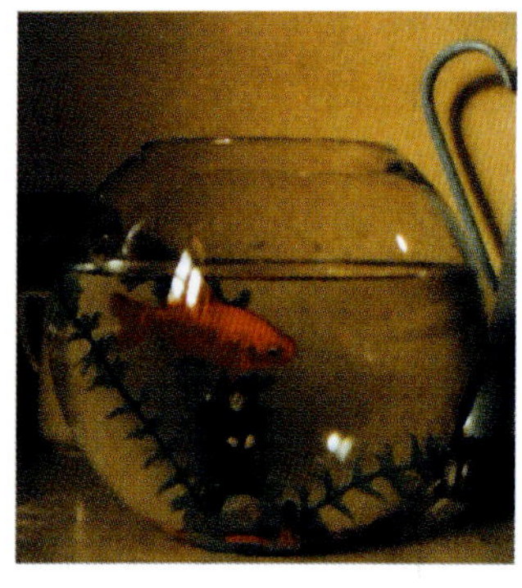

Aquatic animals

The red fish in the film
Amélie (2001)
by Jean-Pierre Jeunet

Although they may all refer metaphorically to an aquatic habitat, none of the objects in this section (with the exception of Gehry's *Pito* kettle) relates directly to water or to the domestic settings associated with the household water supply (the bath, the kitchen sink). The relationship between any of these objects and an aquatic animal exists entirely on a formal level: an armchair seen in profile resembles a cetacean (Erberto Carboni's *Delfino* [Dolphin]); a dish for cooking and serving fish at the dining table is designed like the shell of a bivalve (Roberto Sambonet's *Pesciera* [Fish Dish]);

a table lamp adopts the transparent silhouette of a jellyfish (Olaf von Bohr's *Medusa*); a letter opener made of plastic and steel imitates the opening of an alligator's jaws (Khodi Feiz's *Ali-The-Gator*); an egg beater has plastic strands that resemble the tentacles of an octopus (Marta Sansoni's *Folpo*); a new model for fast-food cutlery has the unmistakable morphology of a mollusk (Giulio Iacchetti and Matteo Ragni's *Moscardino* [Musky Octopus]).

They are liquid shapes and flowing forms. It is as if the typical qualities of animals accustomed to gliding through the water had been preternaturally transferred to these objects, in an interplay of relationships far richer than the mere attribution of a name.

Delfino

Armchair
Erberto Carboni
1954
Arflex

An emblematic example of the so-called "organic" trend in fifties design, Erberto Carboni's *Delfino* (Dolphin) armchair draws its inspiration from the sinuous, flowing forms of the cetacean whose name it bears. Never descending to facile, predictable imitation, it conveys the sculptural perfection of the contours suggested by the world of nature. Viewed in profile, the angle of contact between the parts of its construction (seat, armrest and back) seems to acquire the dynamic impulse of a body thrusting itself upward in a muscular exertion, emerging from the water and balancing in the air. In the blue version, the color of the upholstery reinforces the reference to the aquatic habitat as the genesis of the design's inspiration.

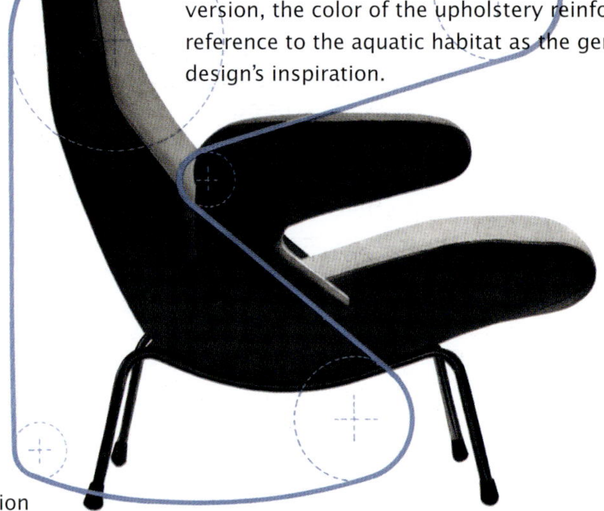

Arflex Collection

16 pesci

Puzzle
Enzo Mari
1973
Danese

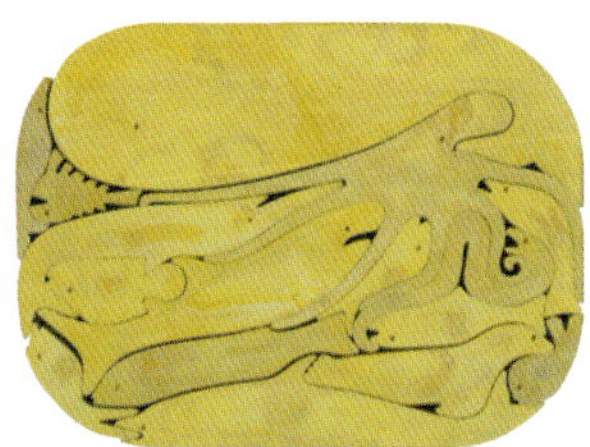

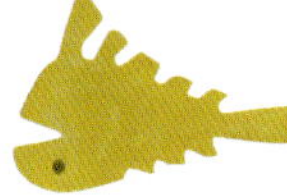

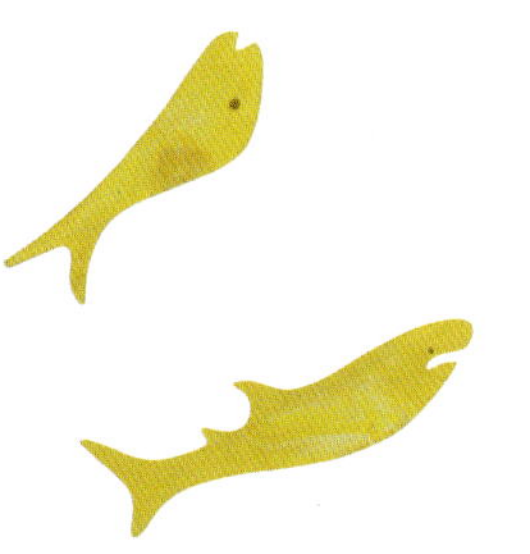

Triennale di Milano Collection

In 1957, with *16 animali* (16 animals) and the *Gioco delle favole* (Game of fables), Enzo Mari had orchestrated the animal world of Aesop's fabulous bestiary. The first of these was a design of inlaid animal forms in wood, that translated the zoomorphic silhouettes best known to children into geometrical forms by means of a subtle and well-balanced relationship between recognizable characteristics (the camel's hump, the elephant's trunk, the giraffe's tail) and abstract elements (determined by the geometry and fit of complementary shapes); in the second design, Mari represented animals by means of precise patches of color, without overburdening them with marks imitating reality.

In *16 pesci* (16 fishes), however, the zoomorphic aspect becomes more explicit, because of the need to enable children to recognize various species of sea creature more easily (the whale, the swordfish, the octopus, the sea snake).

This object should not be confused with a jigsaw puzzle, where each separate piece has no value in itself and must contribute to forming a "sensible" whole. In Mari's game it is the whole that makes no sense (except possibly as a geometric aquarium), and it has to be taken apart so that the individual pieces, transformed by narrative, can produce further possible meanings.

Fish Dish

Roberto Sambonet
Bruno Monguzzi
(packaging)
1957
Sambonet

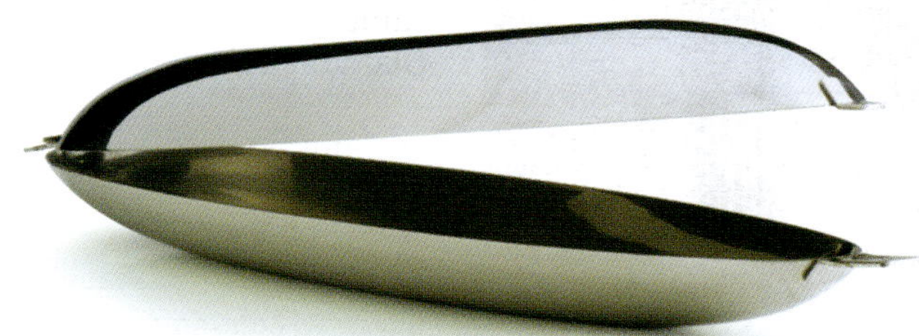

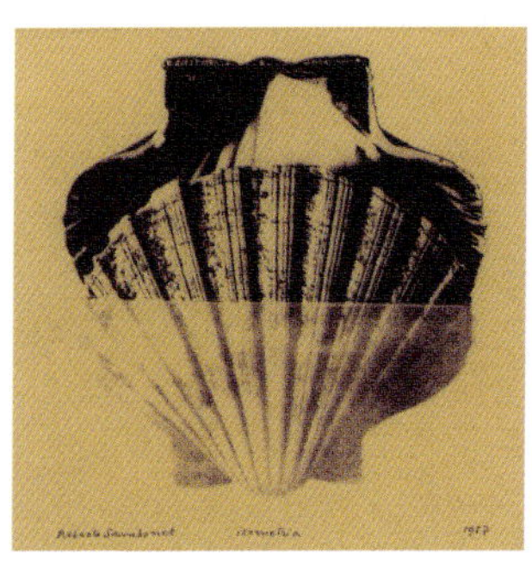

Triennale di Milano Collection

Form as echo, archetype, destiny. In order to design a fish dish (in other words, something that can be used either for cooking a fish in the oven or for serving it at the table), Robert Sambonet drew his inspiration from the quintessential marine shape, the shell of a bivalve. Fabricated from steel, the container is connected with what it is destined to contain, in accordance with one of the ancient relationships of resemblance (*convenientia, aemulatio, analogia, simpatia*) of which Michel Foucault speaks in *The Order of Things*. A fish dish, obviously, could contain anything, not just fish (the two halves, with their simple hinge, can remain open in three different positions, or else they can be separated and used independently). But one could also decide to withhold the object from any functional use, maintaining its purity as an aesthetic object and signifier. As the designer himself points out, it is a sculpture. But it is also a sculpture that can be used.

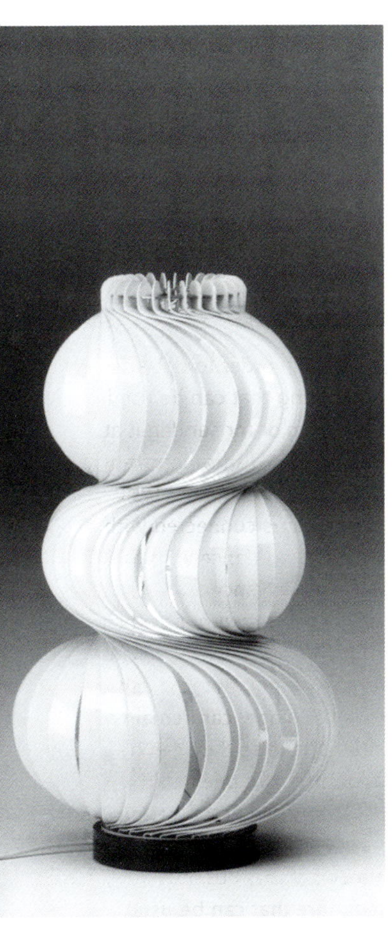

Medusa

Lamp
Olaf von Bohr
1968
Ecolight, later Valenti

Sinuous and spiral-shaped, this lamp by Olaf von Bohr brings to lighting design some of the morphological characteristics of the sea creature from which it takes its name. The light that filters between the lacquered strips gives the illuminating body an almost gelatinous appearance, while the round profile is reminiscent of the shape of a coelenterate swollen with water and plankton. Less likely is a reference to the mythological creature of the same name, who is well known for having turned to stone all those who dared to gaze upon her.

Valenti Collection

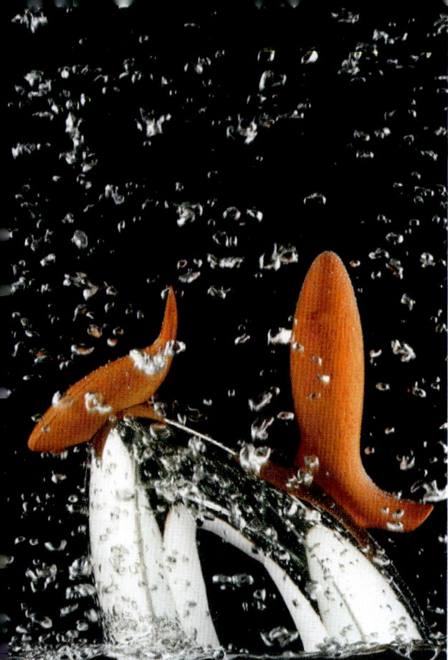

Pito

Kettle
Frank O. Gehry
1992
Alessi

Alessi Collection

One of the themes dearest to Gehry is the fish, a recurrent figure in both his sculpture and his architecture. He placed an enormous one in front of the Fishdance Restaurant in Kobe, Japan; and another, made of wood and without a tail, in Palazzo Pitti; there was yet another in an exhibition in Minneapolis, where he performed an amputation of the fins and head, reducing it to pure essence while retaining its movement. In 1998 Gehry explained: "I began drawing fish. Without any particular purpose, finding that I liked them, that they gave the sense of movement present in the sculptures of Phidias or in certain Indian figures. Or in Bernini, a master at introducing movement into marble." The same thing happens when Gehry approaches design, as in the case of *Pito*, a kettle with a mahogany handle and tuneful whistle, both shaped like little whales, leaping and cavorting on the top. The part that contains the water has two curving segments that make it look very much like the crest of a wave.

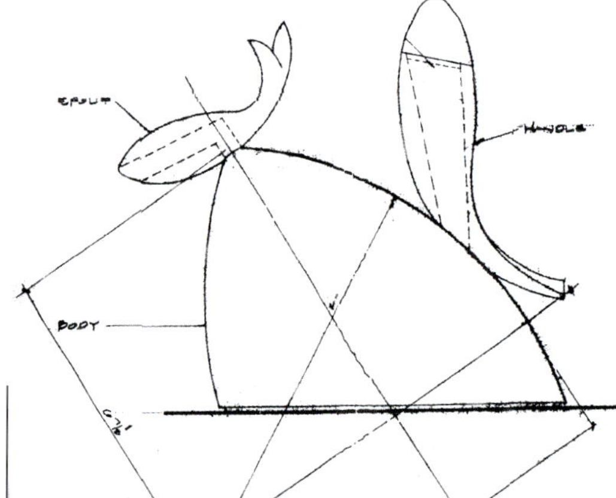

Folpo

Egg beater with measure
Marta Sansoni
1998
Alessi

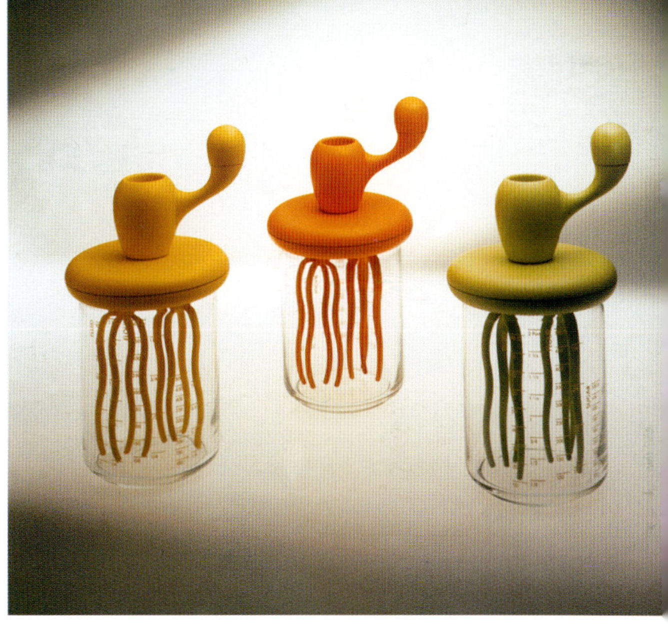

Beating. Whisking. Whipping. In this object designed by Marta Sansoni, the functions generally assigned to metal wires or blades in a traditional beater are instead performed by small strands of plastic that resemble the tentacles of an octopus. In fact, *folpo* means octopus in Venetian dialect: another case in which the object's given name helps to specify the zoological source that inspired its design. Colorful and humorous, decidedly vernacular even in its name, *Folpo* is an easy-going, playful example of the zoophilous genre.

Alessi Collection

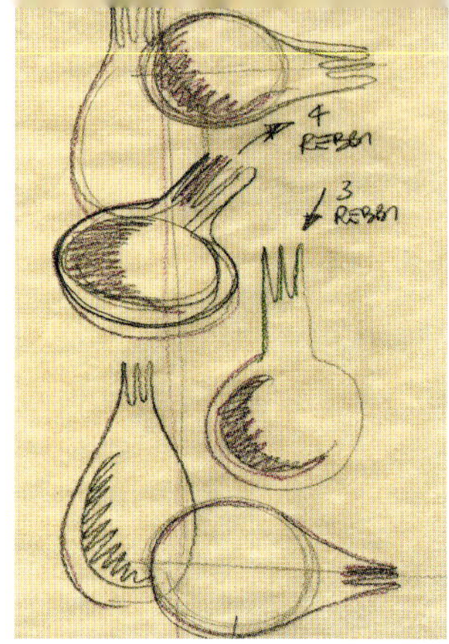

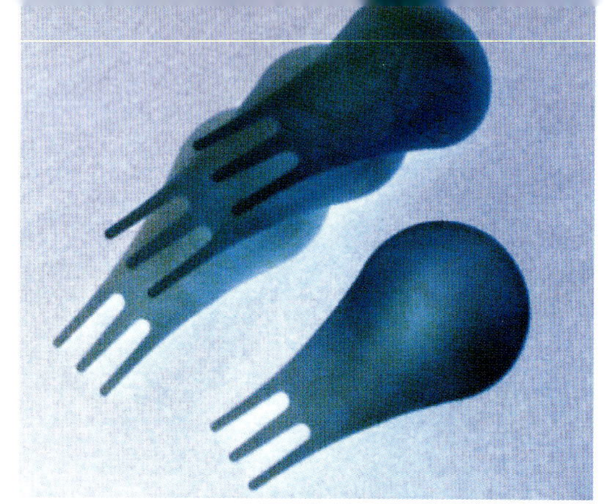

Moscardino

Fork-spoon
Giulio Iacchetti
Matteo Ragni
2000
Pandora Design

Conceived to combine the functions of both fork and spoon, this example of disposable cutlery performs a daring act of crossbreeding by merging into a single artifact two indispensable implements for conveying food to the mouth. The prongs of the fork become the handle of the spoon, which in turn becomes the handle of the fork – a relationship of perfect reversibility. The inventive design responds to changes in dining habits (eating informally, standing up, in a hurry), while on the morphological plane the explicit reference is to a mollusk – the musky octopus that lives in the water. Small in scale, and also suitable for children, it is made of Mater-Bi, a biodegradable plastic obtained from the starch of corn, wheat and potato, manufactured by Novamont, an Italian company that has received international recognition for research and innovation in waste disposal.

Triennale di Milano Collection

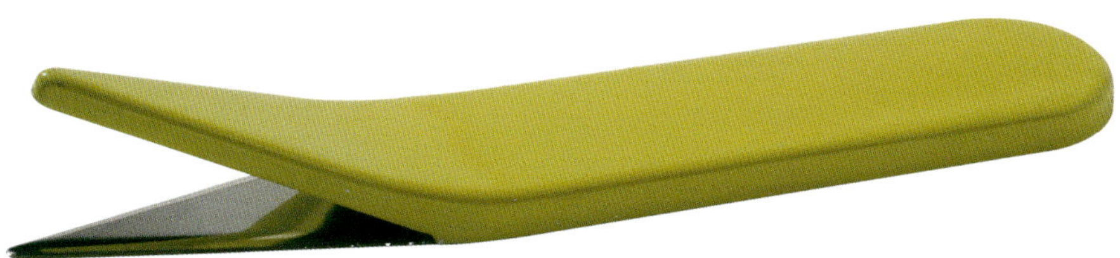

Ali-The-Gator

Letter opener
Khodi Feiz
2001
Alessi

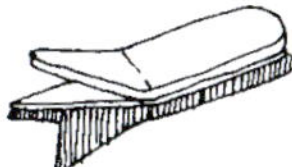

Strange echoes of shapes. Internal rhymes. Playful analogies. What connection is there between a letter opener made of plastic and steel and an alligator? None, apparently. Apart from an echo. A rhyme. An analogical and archetypal reference. The flatness of the reptile's body becomes the object's handle, and the divergence of the gaping, cutting jaws neatly accommodates the cutter's blade. Alessi's zoophilia plays with essential structures, divesting forms of decorative frills and relocating them in new contexts, persuading them to perform new functions. That is how a design's creation originates: from the ability to take a risk, in trying to discover similarities where there seemed to be only radical differences.

Alessi Collection

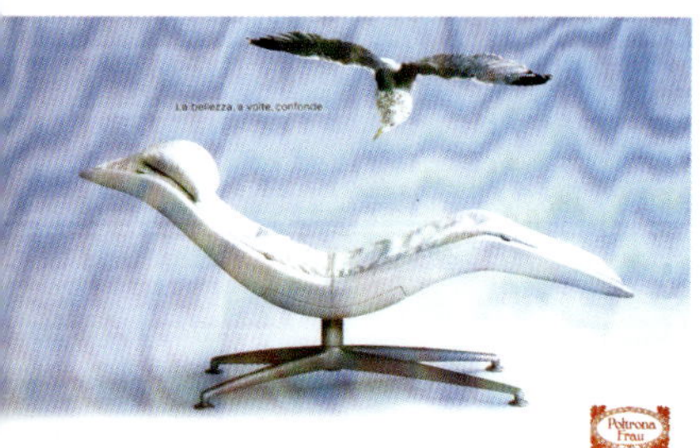

Flying animals

Larus. Frau Research and Development Center.
2001 Advertising campaign, Armando Testa

Sometimes they suggest two wings asymmetrically extended in the act of flying (Tom Dixon's *Bird* lounger). Sometimes they recall an insect of the hymenopter family (the Piaggio *Vespa* [Wasp]), or they evoke the airy grace of a butterfly as in (Alvaro Siza's *Falena* [Moth] lamp, Guido Rosati's *Papillon* [Butterfly] soft chair, and Riccardo Dalisi's *Mariposa* [Butterfly] bench). And sometimes they imbue a domestic object – a lamp, for example – with the unmistakable shape of a gosling, a bat or a heron. All are flying animals – inhabitants of the air. One common element among the styles and models in this section is the idea of lightness, or rather, lift: whether chairs, scooters, tables or lamps, these objects, all named after flying creatures, give the visual impression of wanting to detach themselves from the ground; both in shape and name they convey the archetypal attitude of flight.

Mosquito

Micromotor
Ufficio Tecnico Garelli
1946
Garelli

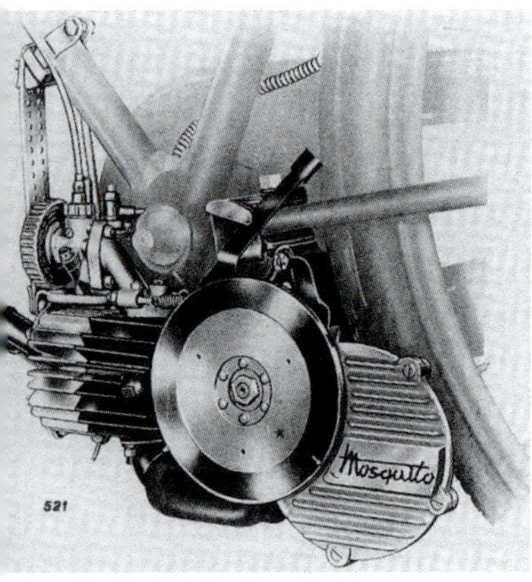

Carlo Civardi Collection

Modeled after the curious collapsible vehicles that were issued to American and British parachutists so that they could move along enemy lines more easily, the Garelli *Mosquito* offered a potentially simple and immediate solution to the need to increase individual mobility during Italy's reconstruction years: the motorization of an ordinary bicycle. The *Mosquito* is, in fact, a small auxiliary motor with a roller-drive that can easily be fitted to any two-wheeler with pedals, providing a range of 60 kilometers on 5 liters of fuel. Like the Ducati *Cucciolo* (Puppy) produced during the same years, the *Mosquito* was a first step towards the motorization of private individuals in a country longing to leave behind the impoverished Neo-Realist atmosphere of *The Bicycle Thief*.

The spread of the *Mosquito* was so rapid and so extraordinary that people began to use the name to indicate any kind of power-assisted cycle.

Coincidentally, the sound produced by the motor in operation is not unlike the buzzing of an insect in flight.

Vespa

Motor scooter
Corradino D'Ascanio
1946
Piaggio

Conceived in 1946 by the helicopter designer Corradino D'Ascanio – who applied to this scooter design the all-in-one structural model used for fuselages in aeronautics – the *Vespa* (wasp) was called thus because of its slender waist and aerodynamic structure, resembling the insect from which it takes its name. Its form immediately arouses wonder and admiration: the motor is not visible, the small wheels are half-hidden, the headlight is mounted on the front mudguard and the rear wheel-covering almost brushes the surface of the road. Young people immediately made it a kind of generational status symbol, and the cinema consecrated its fame as a "cult" object, in films ranging from William Wyler's *Roman Holiday* (1953), in which Gregory Peck runs around Rome on a *Vespa* with a marvelous princess played by Audrey Hepburn on the rear seat, to Nanni Moretti's *Dear Diary* (1994), in which the whole of the first section shows the author-actor intent on weaving through the streets of the capital on a *Vespa*. Still in production over fifty years after it was created, it continues to "buzz" lightly and swiftly through the city streets.

Triennale di Milano Collection

Rondine

Camera
Vico D'Incerti
1949
Ferrania

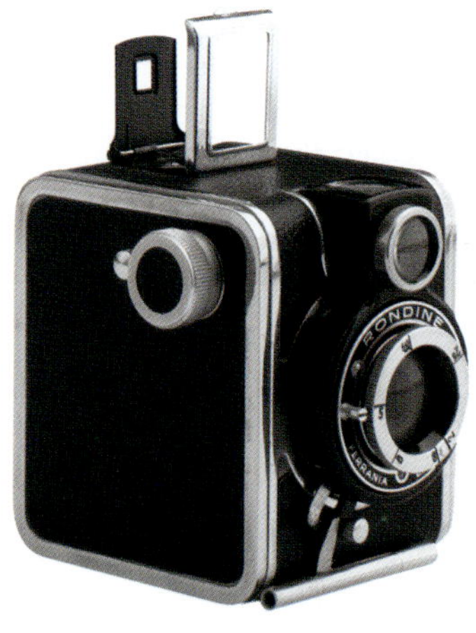

One of the first examples of a cheap, popular camera, Ferrania's *Rondine* (Swallow) helped to spread a massive image-loving culture throughout Italy after the war. To photograph and be photographed thus became not only a way of preserving a visual record of the most important events in one's family life, but also an exercise with which to train one's eye in the emerging realm of audiovisual media. With its modest cost and relative ease of use, it was suitable for anybody: Oliviero Toscani recalls, for example, that *Rondine* was one of the first toys given to him by his parents when he was a little boy. The name can be interpreted either as an example of metonym or as metaphor: in the former case, the allusion is to the black color that this object shares with its namesake, and in the latter the reference is meant to suggest the announcement of a new springtime for the art of photography.

Triennale di Milano Collection

Galletto

Motorcycle
Carlo Guzzi
1950
Moto Guzzi

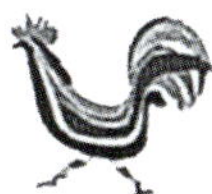

A picture of a small rooster is printed on the front shield that serves to protect the rider from bad weather and accidental injury.

The great novelty of this "light motorcycle" – introduced by Guzzi in 1950 to offer the advantages of both motorcycle and scooter – consists in the posture of the person riding it: no longer straddling, as on a motorcycle, the rider can remain calmly seated, riding in a comfortable, relaxed manner. This is thanks also to the size of the wheels, which offer a good balance between the unduly small wheels of the scooter and the larger wheels used by motorcycles in those years.

The name helps to give the object the uninhibited, gallant and slightly self-important appearance that is typical of the cock, but also mitigated somewhat by the playful familiarity of its diminutive size.

Withdrawn from production in 1966 because of problems in manufacturing, it now has become a coveted collector's item.

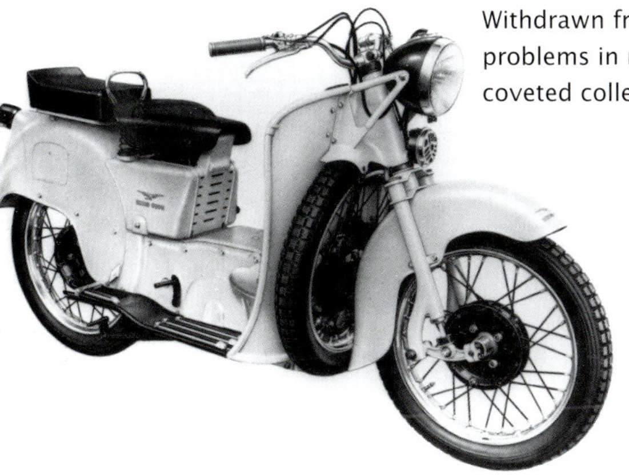

Triennale di Milano Collection

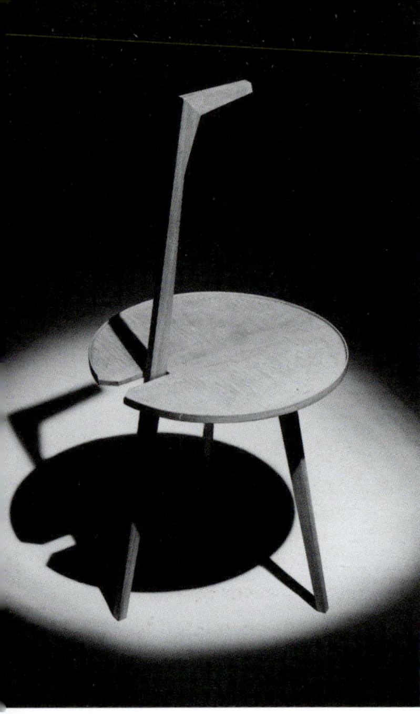

Cicognino

Side table
Franco Albini
1952
Poggi

Objects are often said to be anthropomorphic. Even better, they need to be adapted ergonomically to the shape of the human body. Generally, it's true: designed to accommodate or be of service to the body, to help or support it, everyday objects owe their shape primarily to the need to guarantee a perfectly functional relationship with the morphology and anatomy of the human body.

Sometimes, however, form is detached from function. Or the object manages to perform the prescribed function by assuming a different form. One example is this portable side table designed by Franco Albini in the early fifties. Evocative of the stylized silhouette of a stork, one of its three legs extends into a handle, with the grip, shaped like a neck or beak, positioned precisely at the system's center of gravity. The tabletop, surrounded by a strip of wood, becomes a convenient tray and makes *Cicognino* (Little Stork) an elegantly zoomorphic serving table. It is both a "domestic sculpture" and an abstract signifier full of far-reaching resonances.

Pipistrello

Lamp
Gae Aulenti
1965
Martinelli Luce

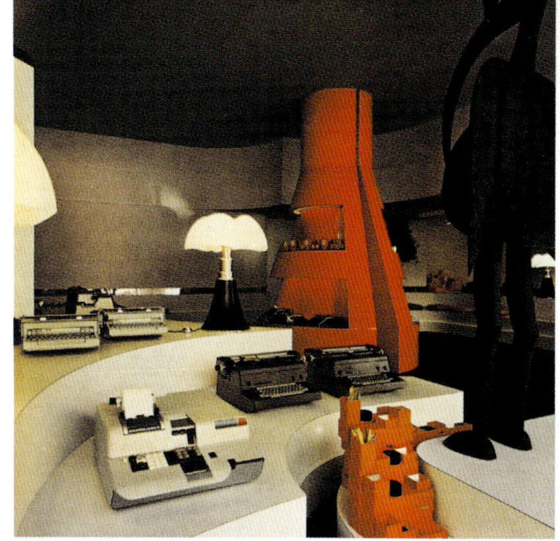

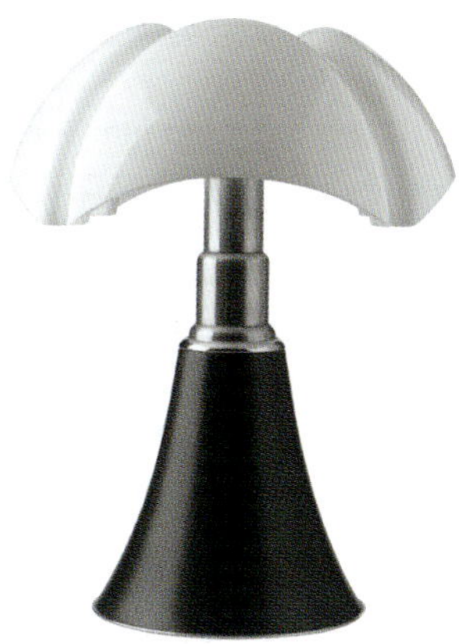

Triennale di Milano Collection

Blending the look of Viennese Secessionism with a rich Pop flavor, the *Pipistrello* (Bat) lamp is related to the nocturnal winged creature by the shape of its white methacrylate diffuser. Resulting from studies of plastic materials and their expressive lighting potential, the lamp has a metal base into which a stainless steel telescopic structure is inserted, making it adjustable in height, and enhancing the overall dimensions and functionality. At the time, these lamps were shown in Olivetti's Paris showroom – redesigned by Gae Aulenti in 1967 – together with various machines displayed on a sort of tiered platform, along with an exotic statue made of African wood.

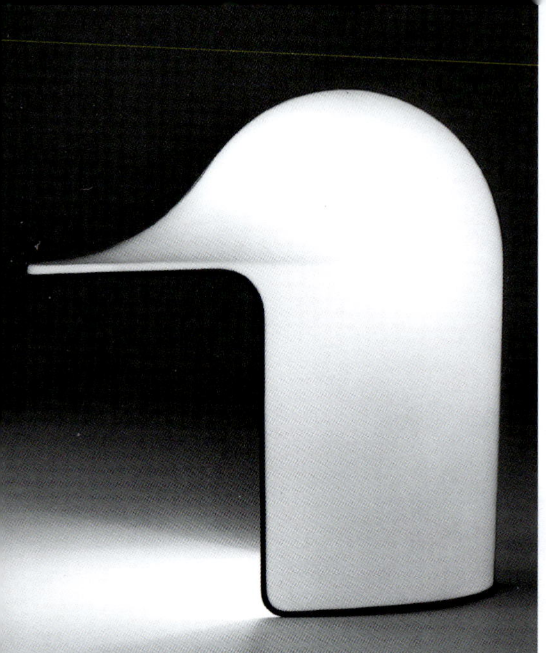 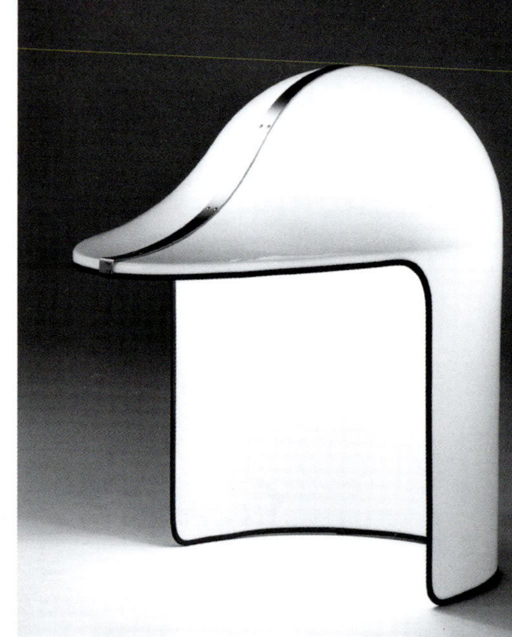

Papero

Lamp
Cini Boeri
1971
Stilnovo

Private Collection

An ancient helm. A covering for the head. A helmet. But full of light. And with an elongated cap, creating the unmistakable shape of the beak of a little goose. *Papero* (Gosling) consists of two pieces of opaline polystyrene connected by a strip of chrome steel with black PVC trim. Designed by Cini Boeri, this floor lamp admirably sums up the ontology of the zoomorphic object, poised between naturalistic echoes, ironic wordplay, nostalgic echoes of vanished artifacts, and innovative, functional design solutions.

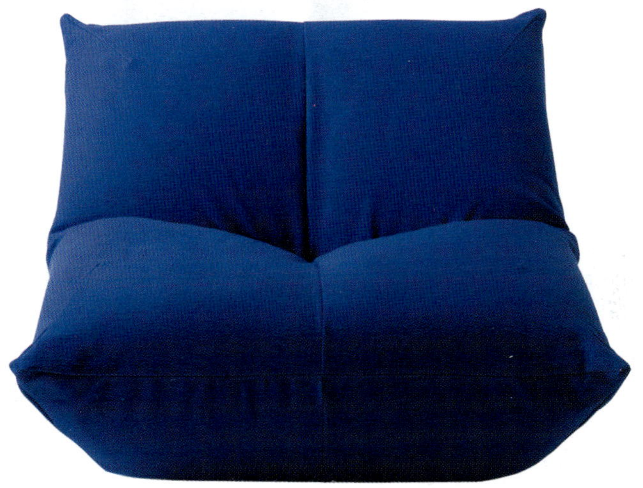

Papillon

Soft chair
Guido M. Rosati
1972
Giovannetti

Triennale di Milano Collection

The symmetrical relationship between the two wings of a butterfly provide the explicit principle behind the composition and design of the *Papillon* (Butterfly) soft chair, designed by Guido Rosati for Giovannetti: the seat and back can be rotated 90° or else inverted so that the back is the seat and vice versa. Influenced by the climate of cultural renewal of the seventies, Rosati dismantled the traditional structure of the armchair as a standard type and unified the functionality of its basic parts, all the while paying tribute to the simplicity and originality of the formal sources that can be found in the animal world.

Mariposa

Bench
Riccardo Dalisi
1989
Zanotta

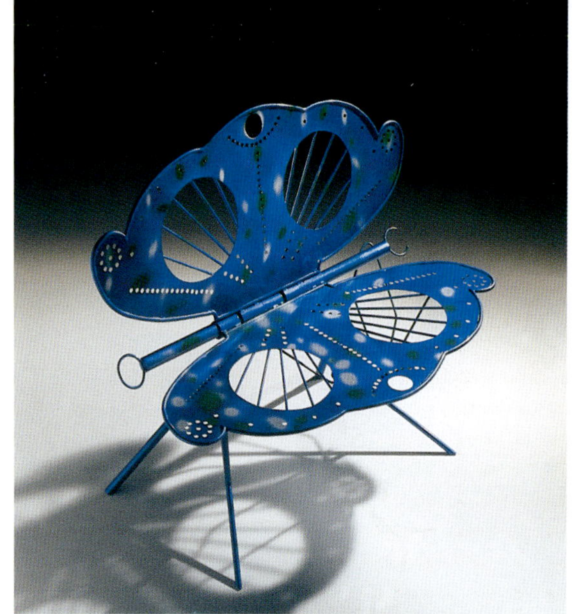

"I always start from something living that is then translated into figures, images, designs. There is nothing more lovely than making something living appear. The whole animate world, the world of living things, is a source of inspiration (including insects, plants and animals). *Mariposa* (Butterfly), 1987, belongs to a group of animal-shaped seats designed initially by Zabro and then by Zanotta: a peacock, a fawn, a little bear, a baby bear cub, and then suddenly, for a side table, a dog (in tinplate) and a Neapolitan mastiff in marble in 1989, and then a crocodile, an elephant, and so on. And also for lighting, later on (1991) I tried making illuminated

Zanotta Collection

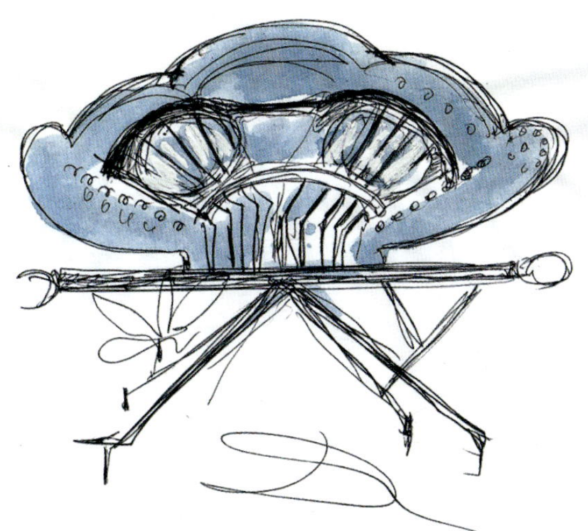

swans, using the *Sister* diffuser and working with O-Luce.
The *Mariposa* was first prototyped with iron rods and
wrought iron; then I thought of offsetting the iron against
sheet aluminum. The first prototype had the two wings
hinged together, so that the back could be placed in
various positions or horizontal.
Why animals? They have a structure and suggest
structure, and also many abstract things are basically
reminiscent of nature: if we remember that Mondrian's
geometrical paintings were derived from a progressive
simplification of the tree we can understand this better..."
(Riccardo Dalisi, April 2002)

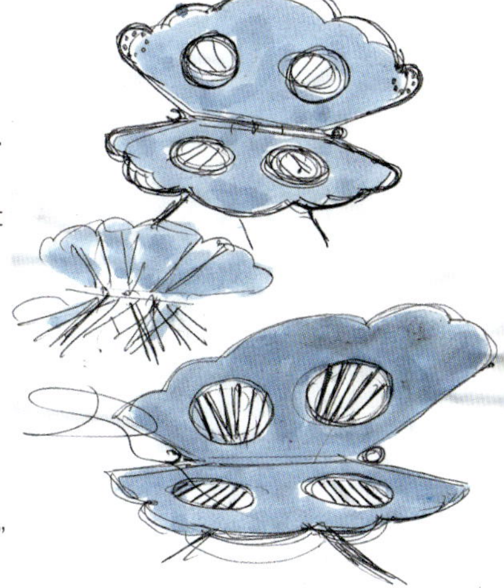

Bird

Chaise lounge
Tom Dixon
1990
Cappellini

"Dixon instills wit into objects and makes them dance." These words by historian Peter Dormer neatly sum up the work of the British designer Tom Dixon, who trained during the era of the London punk rock scene in the eighties. He first made his name as a designer for Disney studios, and later as a creator of objects made from recycled materials.

Attracted by natural forms related to the beginnings of Abstract Expressionist art, Dixon has created seats shaped like leaves (*Fat*, 1988), and objects with distinctly zoomorphic features. *Bird*, with a wood structure and removable cover, belongs to this latter category, its asymmetrical position capturing the opening of the wings of a bird in flight. The angled back recalls a wing raised vertically, while the seat echoes a wing extended horizontally, with the lightness, thrust and energy of flight.

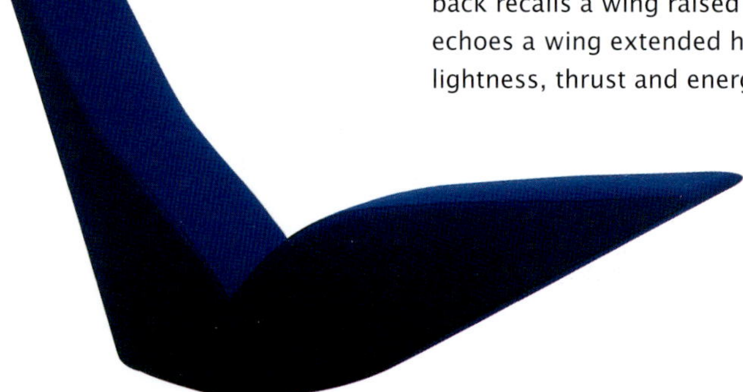

Cappellini Collection

Heron

Lamp
Isao Hosoe
Alessio Pozzoli
1994
Luxo Italiana

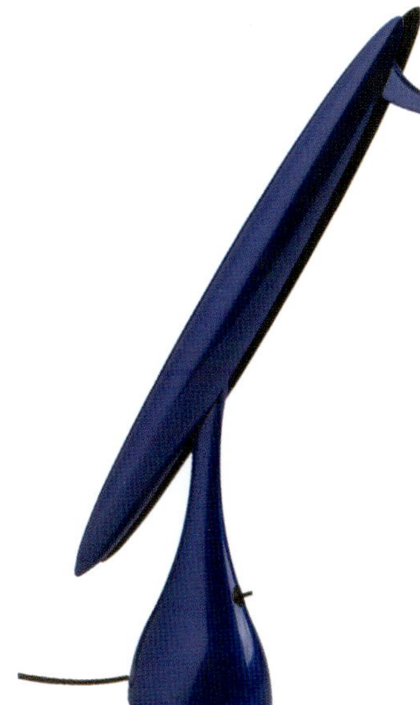

Triennale di Milano Collection

Capable of giving out an asymmetrical light, ideal for an ergonomic work setting and ensuring comfort without tiring the eyes, *Heron* is based entirely on gravitational balance: the structure consists of two parts that can shift forwards and backwards in a way that is reminiscent of the repetitive movements of the heron as it lands on an expanse of water. A pantograph mechanism makes it possible to adjust the angle of the reflector independently of the position of the arm: the result is that the lamp can adopt various "postures," all imitating possible ornithological positions (from gazing across the land to descending in a nose dive).

"Heron loves flying high. He flew so high that one day he left his planet, and when he reached the Earth he became light" (Isao Hosoe).

Falena

Lamp
Alvaro Siza
1994
Fontana Arte

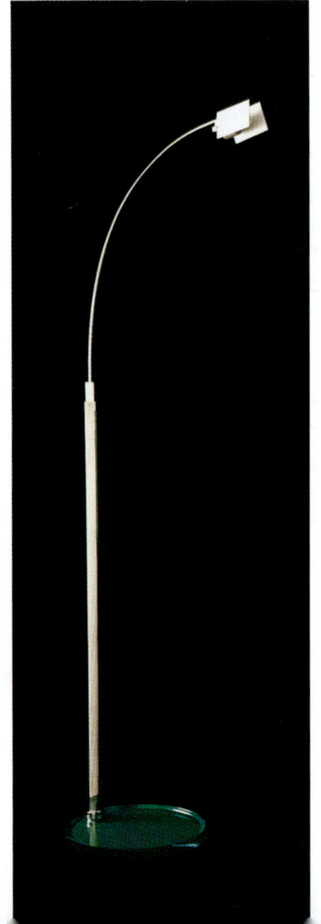

Just as in his architectural works, Alvaro Siza's design activities maintain an attitude that finds its most distinctive characteristics in equilibrium – in an ability to compose shapes with a sober, minimalist essentiality. The *Falena* (Moth) lamp, designed in 1994 for Fontana Arte, confirms this: at the end of a very light, curved stem is a chrome metal lighting unit that can be turned 360˚. The reference to the moth, a winged creature of the night, adds a further technical note to the perfectly discrete design: it is not so much a lamp with a bold design as a restless, almost weightless source of illumination.
Like a flicker of light in the darkness.

Fontana Arte Collection

The Fly

Drawing pins
Donata Paruccini
2001
Alessi

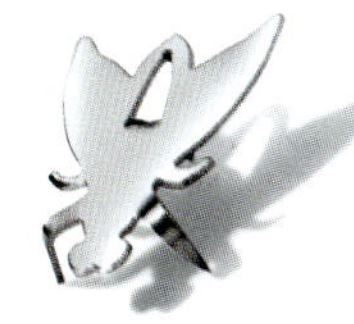

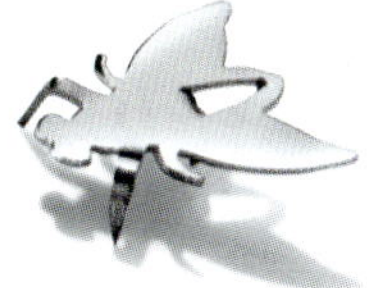

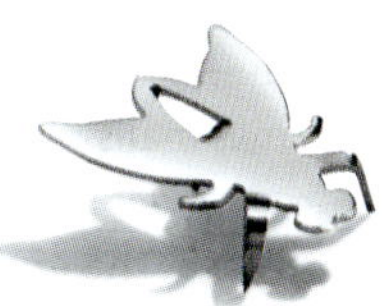

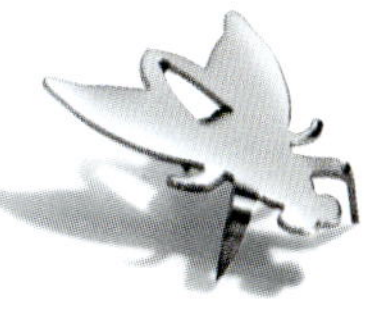

One of the most classic "anonymous objects" – the drawing pin – is brought back into the realm of design by a slight morphological mutation proposed by Donata Paruccini for Alessi: the traditionally round head acquires the flattened outline of a fly with wings extended, while pointed pins occupy the position of the insect's legs. Perhaps we lose something of the archetypal perfection of the traditional drawing pin (a "spontaneous" form, Bruno Munari would have said, "dictated by clarity and economy of construction"), but the gesture revisits the object with the necessary irreverence that never takes any form for granted or treats it as eternal.

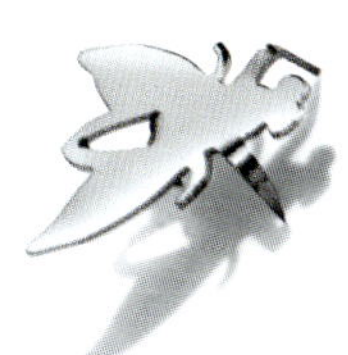

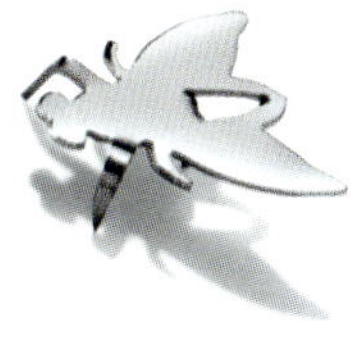

Alessi Collection

Animals of play and fantasy

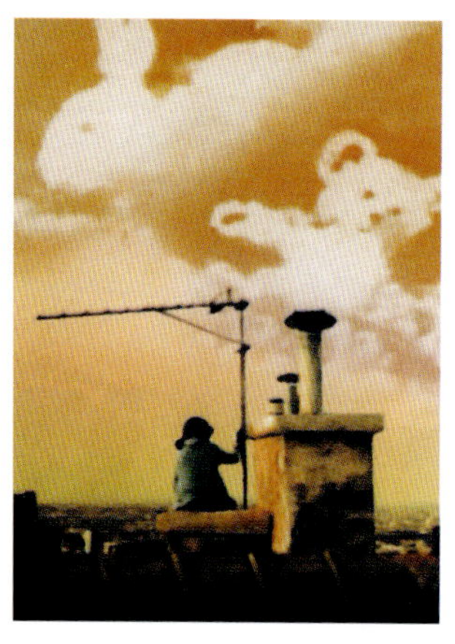

Rabbit and teddy bear-shaped
clouds in the film
Amélie (2001)
By Jean-Pierre Jeunet

For the objects in this section, the zoomorphic classifications and designs perform a reworking on a secondary level: they do not confine themselves to evoking the common name of an animal species but refer instead to entities already accepted in the world of the imagination, already endowed with an identity of their own. Or else they generate new artifacts that serve to enrich the range of possible objects – not so much within the sphere of the *useful* as that of the *playful*. In the first case, objects obtain their names in a conscious process of post-modern crossbreeding between highbrow references and lowbrow "pop": from literature (*Moby Dick*), from mythology (*Chimera*), from comic strips (*Snoopy*, *Fritz the Cat*), from cartoons (*Bibip*), or from advertising (*Calimero*). In the second case, however, it is the imagination of the designer that gives life to the object (Munari's cat *Meo Romeo* and his little monkey *Zizì*, Philippe Starck's *Juicy Salif* lemon juicer, Denis Santachiara's *Notturno italiano* [Italian nocturne] lamp), making them available for playful interaction or imaginative reinterpretation. The roles of imagination and play cascade into the world of mass production and leave objects suitable not only as utilitarian artifacts, but also as implements for exercising the imagination. Within these objects, "useful" and "playful" cease to be antithetical categories, finding a meeting-place, a point of exchange and osmosis. Even, perhaps, a moment of coincidence or contiguity.

Meo Romeo

Toy
Bruno Munari
1949
Pirelli

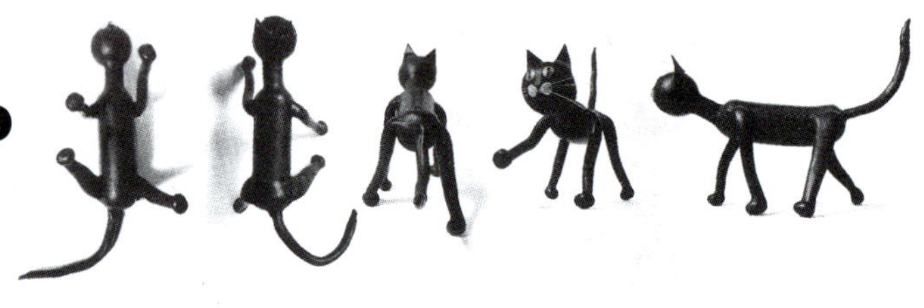

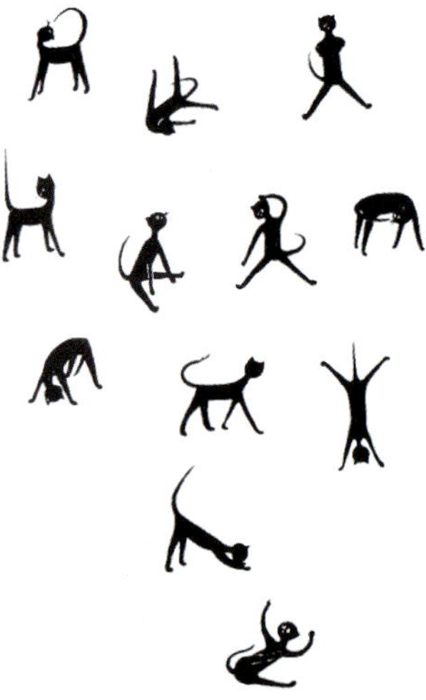

Anty Pansera Collection

In the years immediately after the war, Munari was commissioned by Pirelli to think of a new industrial use for a material that at that time was innovative: foam rubber. The artist had the idea of reinforcing the material with thin copper wire and using it to create a series of children's toys. Munari describes the evolution of the design as follows: "An ordinary piece of foam rubber, in the hands of a child, communicates the softness and elasticity of the material, which seems alive and which, for a child, brings to mind the sensation that one feels when holding a kitten or some other small animal. So I tried to think of toys made of foam rubber and, of course, I became interested in the technological aspect of how to make objects with foam rubber: what the mould should be like, what could be inserted into the material so that the object could be manipulated, and even if it was possible to give the toy a pleasant smell" (Bruno Munari, *Codice ovvio*, Einaudi, Turin 1994). That is how *Meo Romeo* was created: a marriage of technical know-how, playful imagination and zoological charm. Even Picasso is said to have owned one.

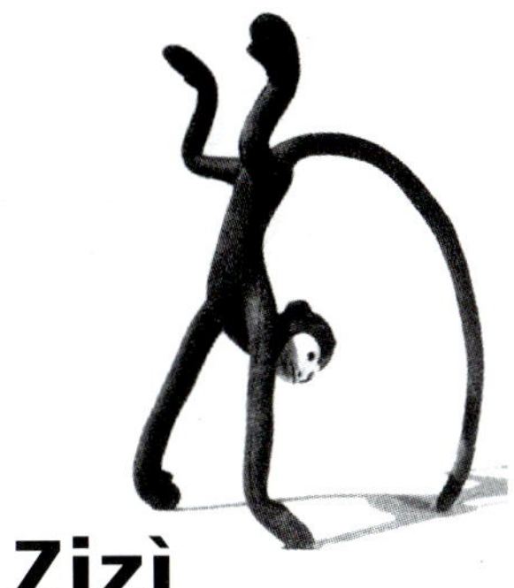

Zizì

Toy
Bruno Munari
1952
Pigomma

A little monkey called *Zizì*, imprisoned in a cellophane packet on which a picture of a wire mesh of a cage is printed, is simply asking to be freed in order to perform all sorts of movements and acrobatics. After an inert period in toy manufacturing in the early fifties, *Zizì* – and the cat *Meo Romeo* – constituted a kind of revolution. This was immediately appreciated by the members of the Compasso d'Oro jury, who in 1954 awarded a prize to Munari's monkey on the following grounds: "Toys are normally 'realistic' or infantilized reductions of mechanical devices, or else imitations, equally realistic or treated with childish irony, of animals or human figures. This little monkey, however, designed by Munari and manufactured by Pigomma, represents an interpretation of a personality – a 'character' that has achieved an essentiality of form with the use of a common material – foam rubber articulated with steel wire reinforcement – providing the enjoyment of endless characteristic positions."

Galleria del Design e dell'Arredamento Cantù Collection

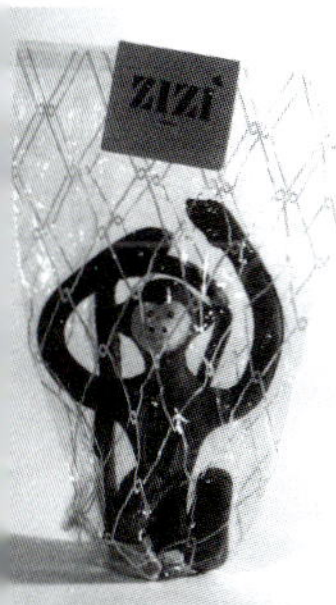

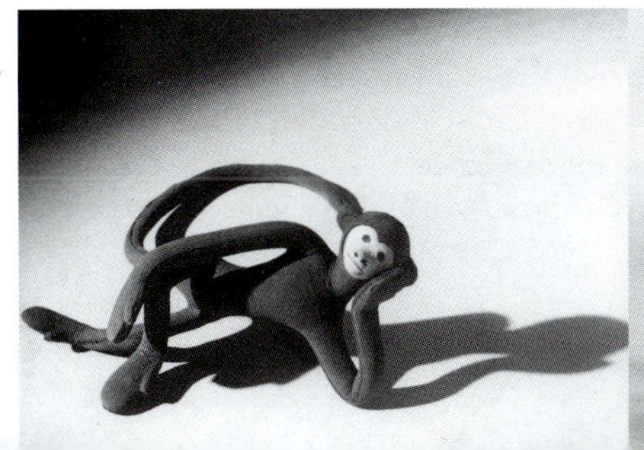

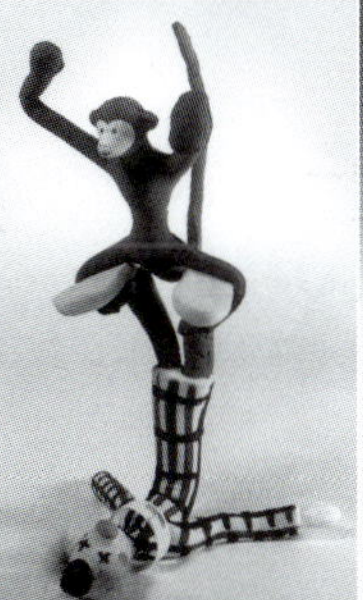

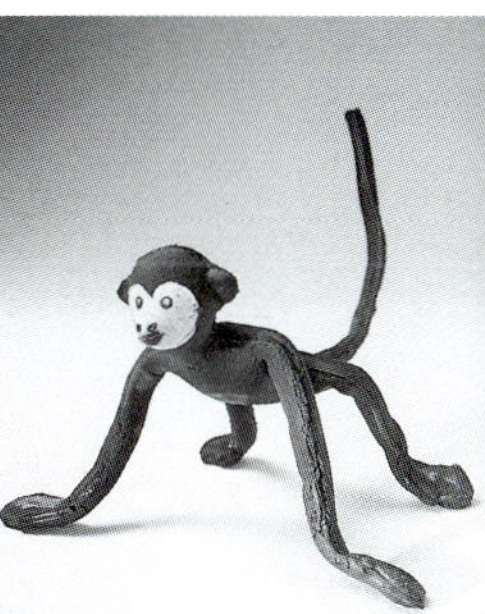

Chimera

Lamp
Vico Magistretti
1966
Artemide

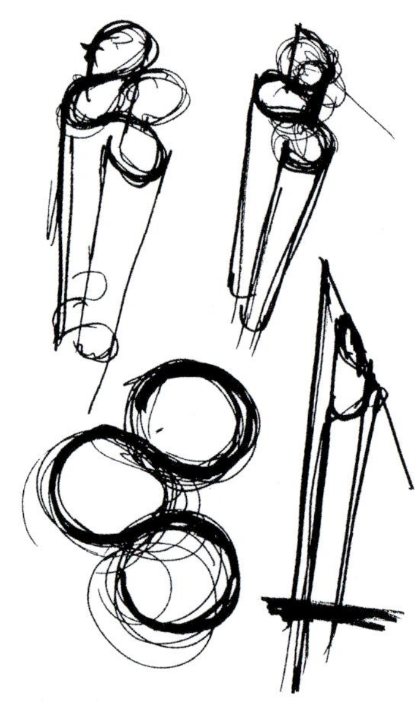

Artemide Collection

Voluptuous and seeming to wrap around itself, this lamp, manufactured by Artemide in the mid-sixties, neatly sums up Vico Magistretti's explorations focused on "using plastic materials in accordance with their characteristics of resistance, constructing the form on the basis of the curvature required to make the surfaces rigid" (Fulvio Irace and Vanni Pasca, *Vico Magistretti*, Electa, Milan 1999, p. 134). In this particular case, the opaline sheet of methacrylate that acts as a light diffuser is made self-supporting by its serpentine configuration. The name refers to the monster of Greek and Roman mythology that the poets described as having the head of a lion, the body of a goat and the tail of a serpent: an impossible and clearly fantastical form, with the result that the word "chimera" has become part of ordinary language to indicate an absurd hypothesis or an empty dream. But in the years leading up to 1968, chimeras and utopias were in fashion with the generation that "dreamed the impossible," and likewise did Magistretti's design provide a contribution to research that made possible the creation of new forms by the use of new technologies applied to new materials.

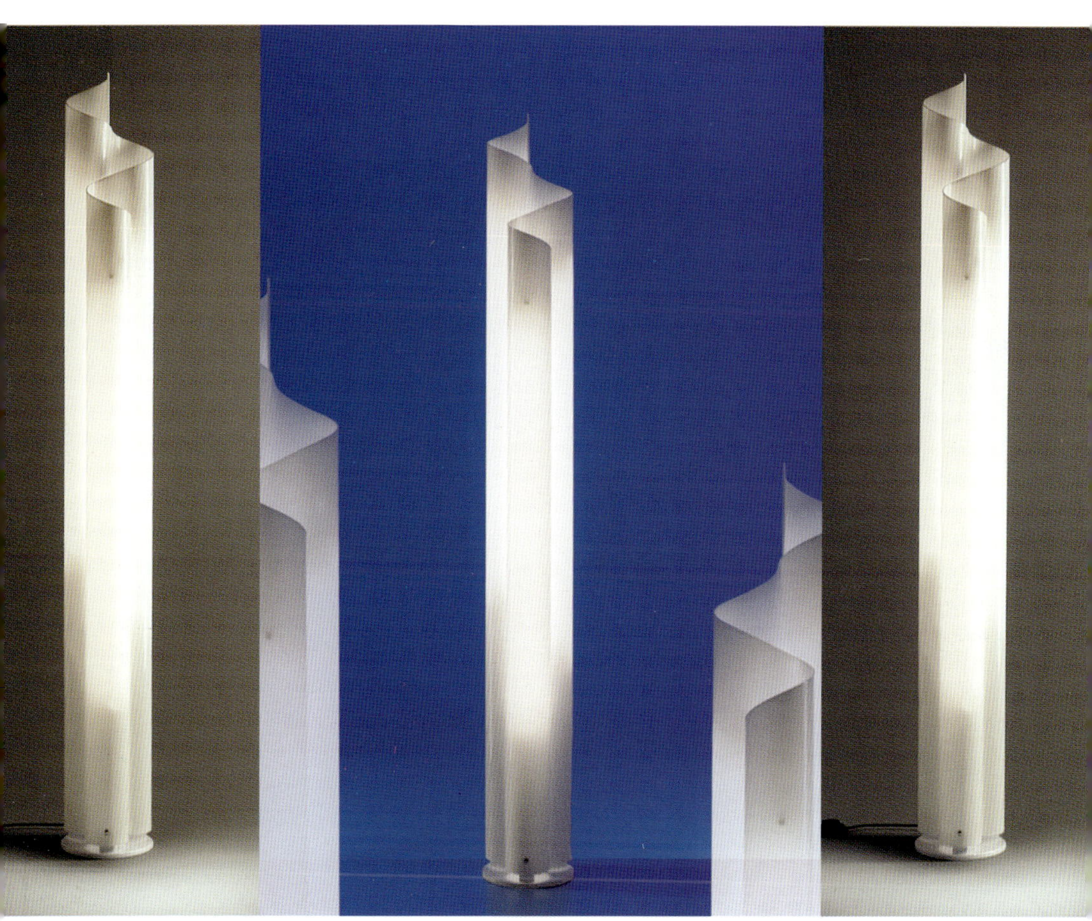

Snoopy

Lamp
Achille and Pier Giacomo
Castiglioni
1967
Flos

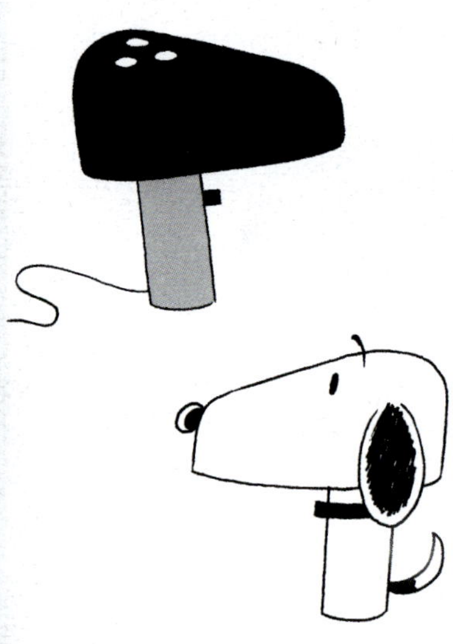

"A dissociated personality if ever there was one, he would like to be an alligator, a kangaroo, a vulture, a penguin, a snake... He tries all the paths of mystification and then surrenders to reality." That is how Umberto Eco – in *Apocalypse Postponed (Perspectives)* – describes Snoopy, the canine antihero of Charles M. Schulz's *Peanuts*. When Eco was writing this in 1964, he could not know that a little later (in 1967, to be precise) Snoopy was to introduce his talent for transformation into the world of objects, in an attempt to become a lamp. In Achille Castiglioni's design there are references to Schulz's cartoon character in the prominent muzzle evoked by the aluminium reflector, and in the slant of the cylindrical base of veined white marble, set at an angle to the plane on which it rests, as if seeking to give the object an impression of apparent instability, very much in keeping with the tone of Schulz's cartoon stories. The lamp is really very stable, as a result of the correct distribution of the weight of the marble base, complemented by the thick sheet of glass that supports the reflector. As in the world of *Peanuts*, Castiglioni's designed "instability" is only a mask behind which hides an object with a personality that is always very clear and well defined. Just like Snoopy.

Flos Collection

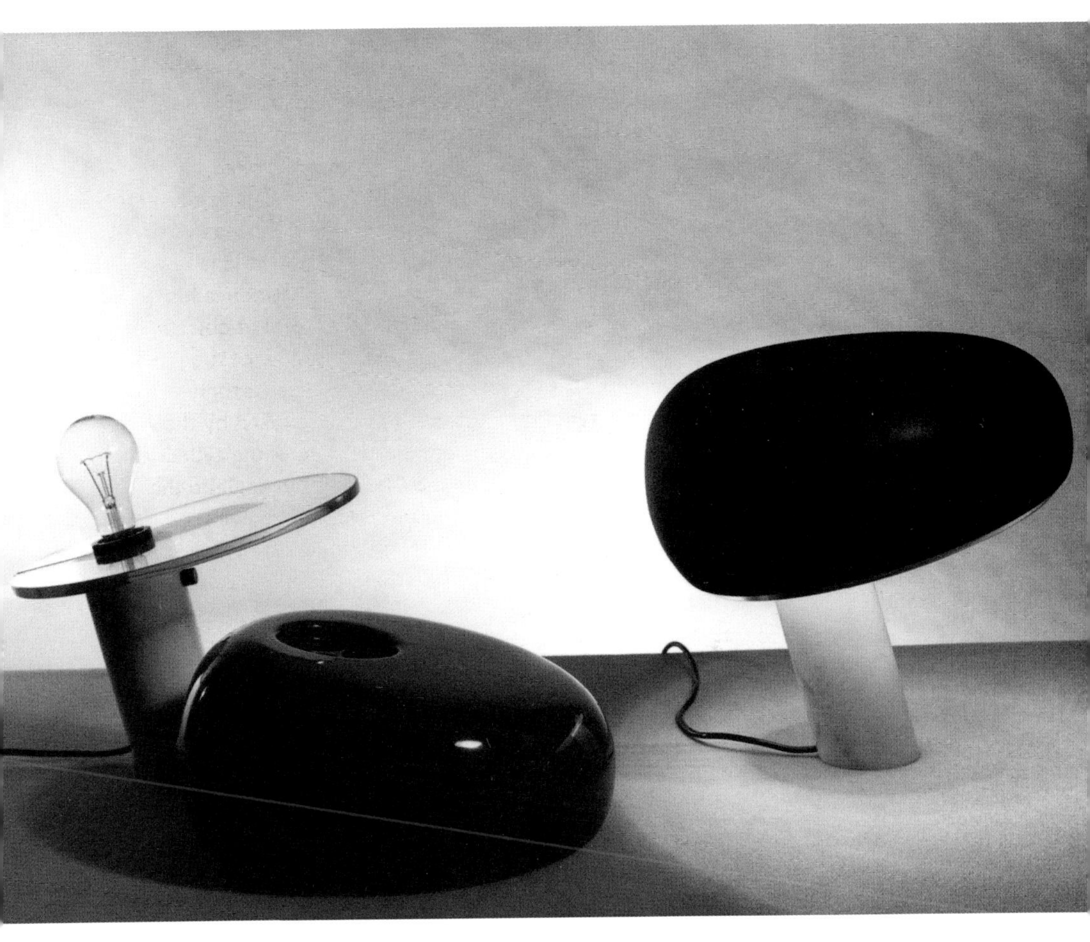

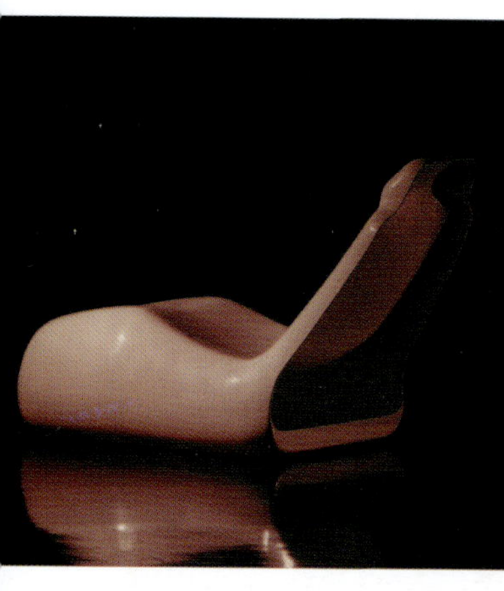

Moby Dick

Chair
Alberto Rosselli
1974
Saporiti

In Herman Melville's immortal pages, Moby Dick "is all things to all men": monster or mystery, devil or god, nature or culture, attraction or repulsion. Something analogous can be said of this chair designed by Alberto Rosselli in 1974: conceived explicitly as a "form with various possible uses" – in other words as a seat that can be set in various positions and has a structure endowed with various "lines of resistance" – Moby Dick is a classic "polysemous object." It is almost an open artwork, or a "formless form" – part cetacean, part monster – that releases the user's imagination and prompts him to try new, unprecedented postures. What is certain is that, when one is reclining on the shell-shaped casing of this strange chair, it is hard for anyone to resist the temptation to feel that they are, as it were, in Captain Ahab's shoes. But at home, rather than amid the billows of the stormy ocean.

Giovanna Ponti Rosselli Collection

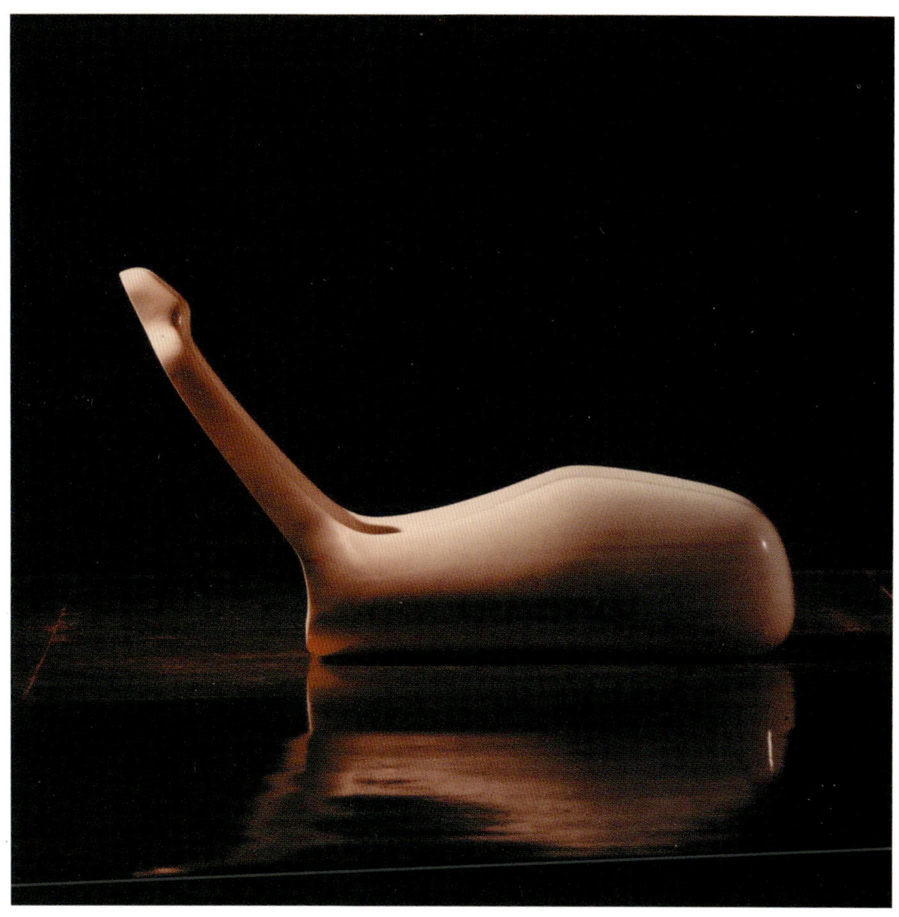

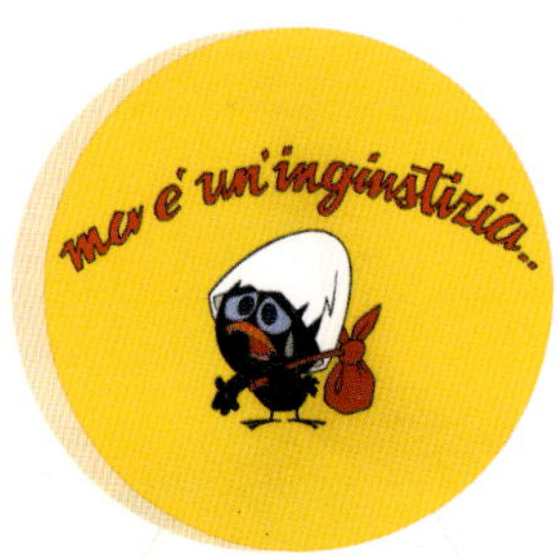

Calimero

Container
Artigiani Comacini
1974
Zanotta

Calimero was first manufactured in 1974, the very year that marked the disappearance from the Carosello TV program of the legendary "little black" chick designed 13 years earlier by Nino and Toni Pagot to advertise a detergent made by Mira Lanza. This series of plant tubs and containers, manufactured by Zanotta, seems to want to bring back to life, through the world of objects, one of the symbols of advertising culture most deeply rooted in the Italian collective imagination. In fact, the icon of the Carosello chick ties in not only with the name and black color, but also with the scampish appearance of these objects, their considerable understatement and, above all, the structure of water-repellent fiber: like an ironic wink recalling Calimero's characteristic aversion to water in advertisements for detergent ("You're not black, you're just dirty…!").

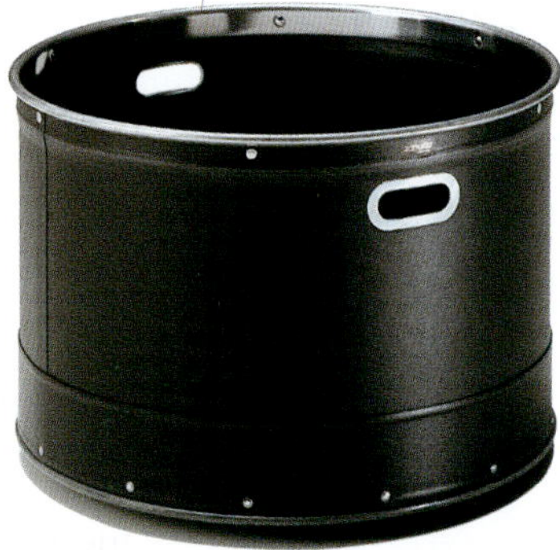

Zanotta Collection

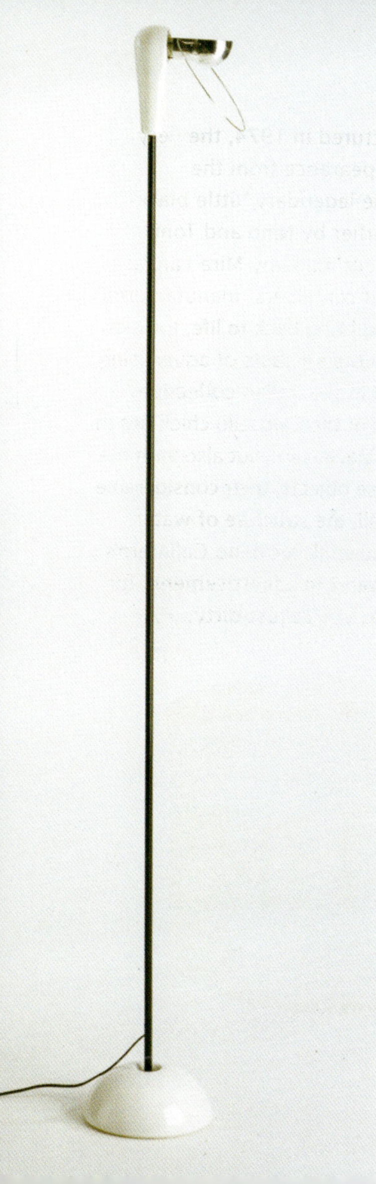

Bibip

Lamp
Achille Castiglioni
1976
Flos

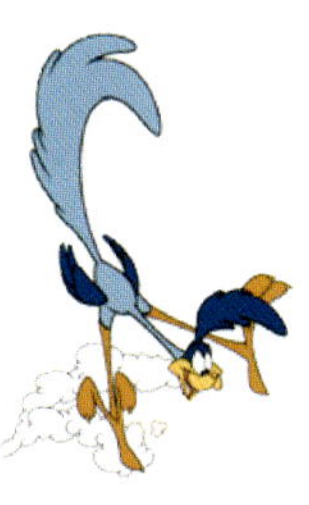

Bibip, a floor lamp with an adjustable light source, stabilized by a hemispherical ceramic base filled with sand, was inspired directly by the celebrated cartoon film created by Chuck Jones for Warner Brothers in 1948, in which a very hungry, solitary predator (Wile E. Coyote) eternally pursues Road Runner, a kind of desert bird capable of supersonic speed, known for the "beep-beep" that he emits from time to time. The painted metal stem and the pressure die-cast, aluminum, rotating reflector give Castiglioni's lamp a profile that openly recalls Chuck Jones's feathered friend. The reference is not only ironic and playful, but also related – after a fashion – to method and design: in fact, both the design and the animated cartoon take place in a world of serial production, each in its different way. Chuck Jones, in particular, is constantly faced with the rules of serial output, seeking to "repeat the same structure endlessly, only altering appearances by the minimum amount that will make the repetition stimulating and not tedious" (Giannalberto Bendazzi, *Cartoons*, Marsilio, Venice 1988, p. 186).

Triennale di Milano Collection

Fritz the Cat

Lamp
King & Miranda
1987
Arteluce, Flos

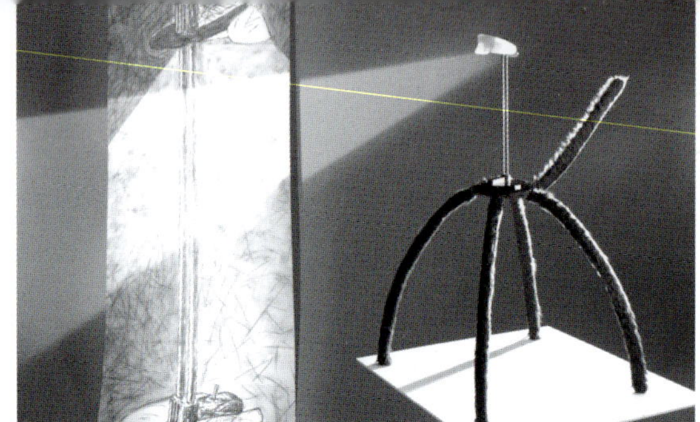

Inspired by a character in Robert Crumb's similarly titled underground comic, King & Miranda's lamp absorbs its ironic, transgressive impulse: like the feline seducer and *bon vivant*, brought to the cinema screen in 1971 in a cartoon by Ralph Bakshi, this lamp also intervenes in the vocabulary of traditional lighting technology and presents itself as an example of the designer's desire to become a "promoter of design in which what matters is the balance between the elements of imagination and those of technical and methodological knowledge" (Gillo Dorfles). A centerpiece of the traveling exhibition *Lonely Tools*, presented in Barcelona, Amsterdam and Tokyo in 1990/91, *Fritz the Cat* is an emblematic example of King & Miranda's "solitary utensil": "Contrivances glorious as wings or humble as crutches that vex us, accompany us, and after we have gone are the only evidence of our passing."

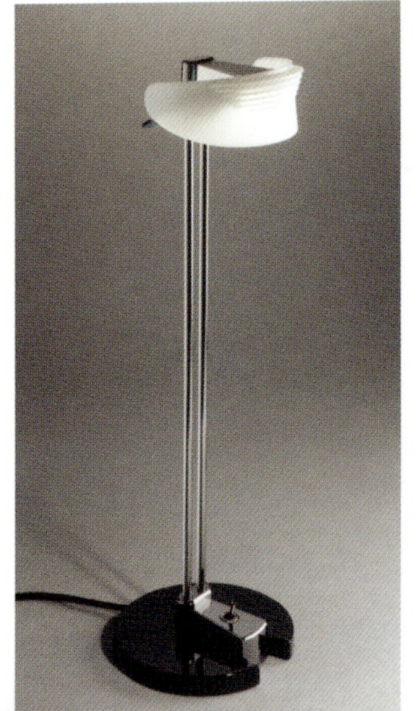

Flos Collection

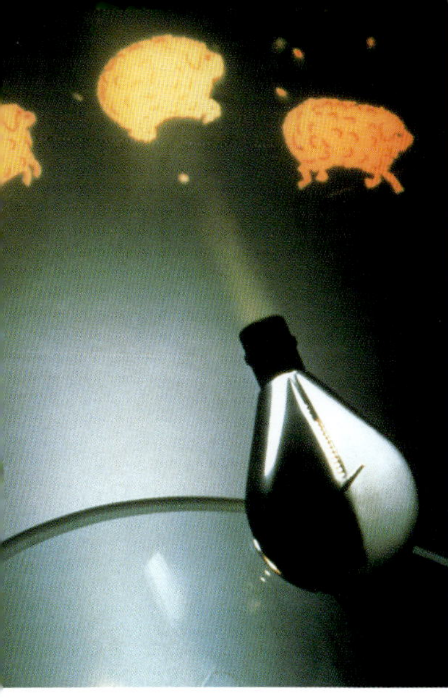

Notturno italiano

Lamp
Denis Santachiara
1988
Modular Domodinamica

An ancient saying declares that in order to fall asleep one must count sheep. And Denis Santachiara immediately comes to our aid in fostering slumber and dreams: the beam of light of his *Notturno italiano* (Italian nocturne) lamp projects sheep continuously, endlessly passing across the wall.

In this case, and throughout all his explorations, Santachiara works with animation, performance, mutation and interaction. Even with a doormat such as *Cicalino* (Little Cicada), he is able to restore to an ordinary object the value and concept of "threshold" by means of a little bird that welcomes you with its twittering. As he himself has said: "Sometimes there is an unfounded pretension that objects are almost like subjects, and hence the attempt to give them names that have some meaning in relation to their body or their spirit... When I am able to give the name myself, I choose something that has to do with humanity as a whole, with the arts and crafts of humanity, or else with personal things. Because there are also names like that, names that are the result of a poetic text, such as *Notturno italiano*" (in *Lezioni di design*, installment no. 10)".

Triennale di Milano Collection

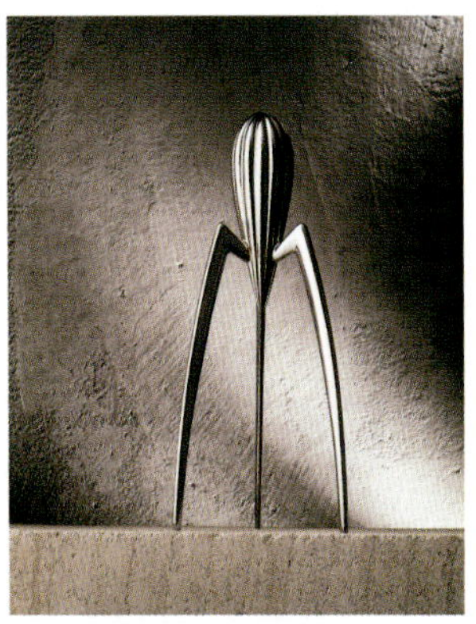

Juicy Salif

Lemon juicer
Philippe Starck
1990
Alessi

Alessi Collection

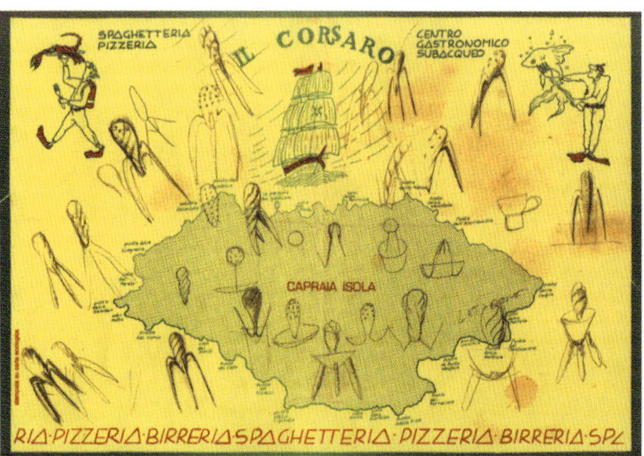

This design was created almost by chance. In a restaurant on the island of Capraia, Philippe Starck was struck by the shape of the octopuses on his plate. He made a drawing of them on the pizzeria's paper place mat and sent it to Alessi. That is how Juicy Salif originated: it looks like a polyp, but it could also be a mutant insect, some unknown species of crustacean or even a Martian. Made of cast aluminum with polyamide legs, it has a minor imperfection on the functional level (the absence of a filter mesh means that the seeds of the fruit fall into the glass along with the juice), but it makes up for this with its power as an "aesthetic object" that escapes mere functionality and projects itself into a fertile dimension that populates a domestic setting with distant echoes and images.

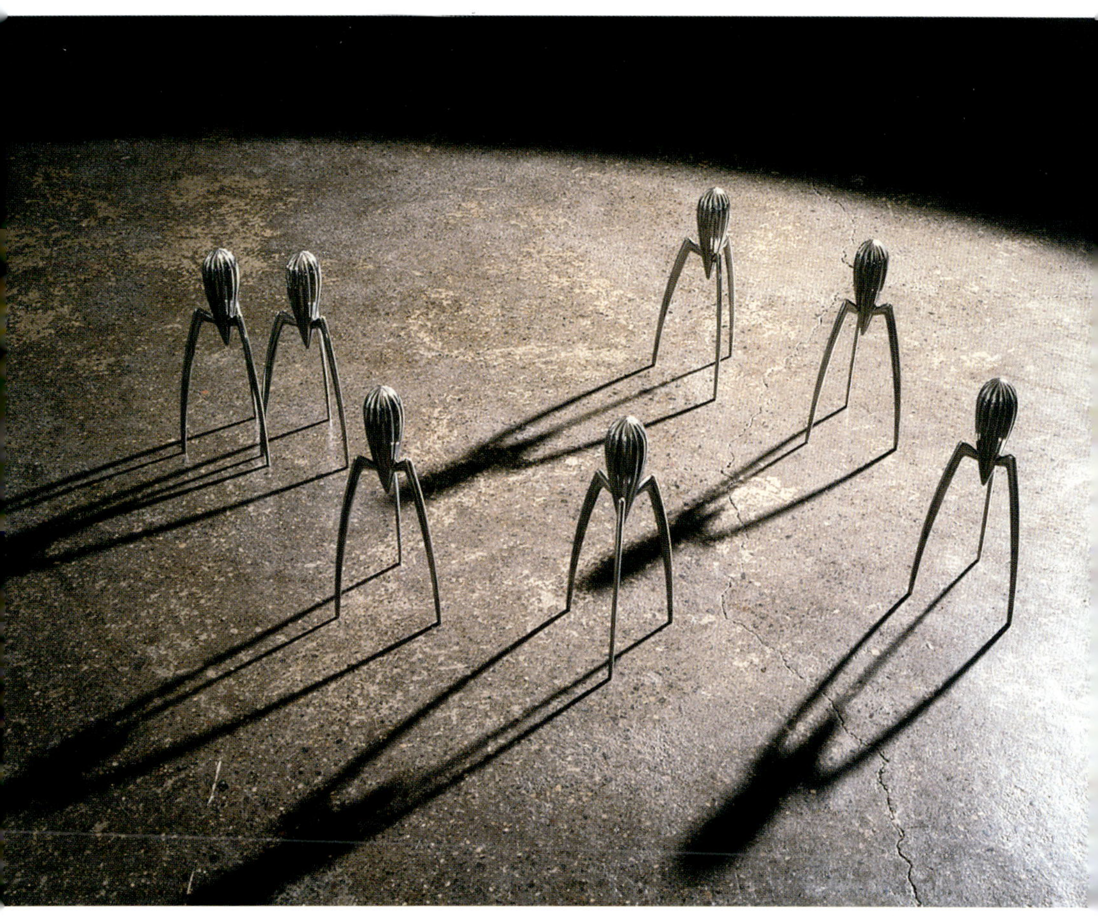

*By a designer to whom fate
has bestowed the name of an
animal, a testimony about
how a domestic animal can
inspire or stimulate the
planning of an object.*

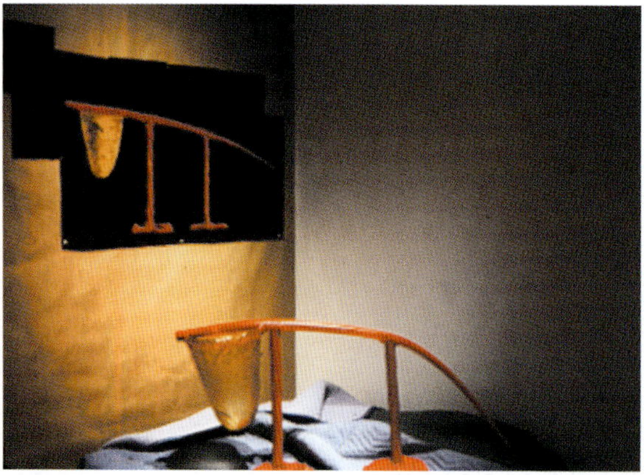

TK

Gaetano Pesce

She has been a powerful presence in one part of my life: during the last nine years and three months. *TK* is a dog. Many people have expressed in word and deed almost everything about the qualities and the magnificent moments that pets have given them. So I shall not do the same. Instead, as *TK* forms part of my general activities, I felt it right and proper to recall her in my work, with an object. I made it about six years ago: it was a flower vase made of elastic urethane.

I am writing these lines at the close of the *Salone del Mobile* in Milan in 2002. There I saw considerable energy among the public, which gets bigger every year, indicating that the culture of the object is capable of becoming an ever vaster and fresher expression.

Yet at the Salon I found very little true creativity. Most of those involved in creation, even the best architects and designers, old and young, are still at what I see as the stage of "decoration." This occurs, unfortunately, with the aid of curatorial institutions and galleries that, if they do not steal, are devoid of curiosity, like a Dutchman who does not know how to fly.

It seems to me that planners and designers have not yet realized that the age of the standard has been superseded, and that the works of architecture and objects that are produced must not only take account of "functionality" but also express the political, religious and existential vision of their authors. They must be documents of our time, of our sorrows, of our joys and feelings. And so the generosity of *TK* also comes into the picture, especially now when, with her white beard, she reminds me of the waning of our "precious days."

April 2002

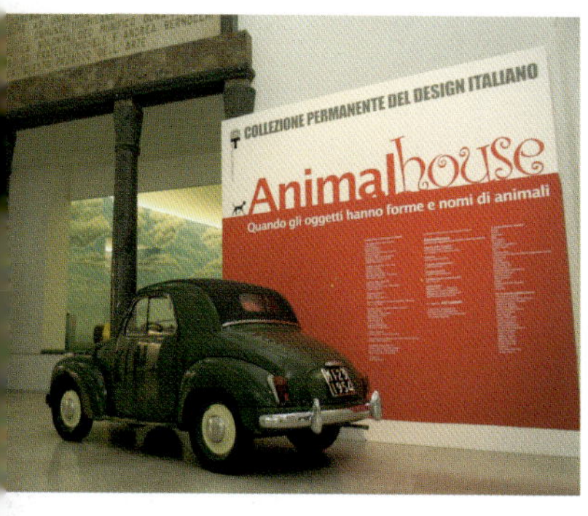

Setting Up

Giancarlo Basili

Giancarlo Basili (1952) is one of the most important set designers in Italian cinema. He has worked with, among others, Gabriele Salvatores (*Nirvana*), Gianni Amelio (*Cosi ridevano*) and Nanni Moretti (*Palombella Rossa, La Stanza del figlio*).

A kind of virtual zoo... A place intended to accommodate different species of animals.

A setting capable of containing within itself the various elements of nature – water, air, sky, earth – in a spectacular way. In other words, a place where one could fly, float or hover.

I conceived the setting of the exhibition *Animal House* as a kind of huge aquarium in which the floor becomes the surface of the sea and the walls are a boundless sky.

The floor was specially made by Abet Laminati, using a retouched, reworked photograph: digital

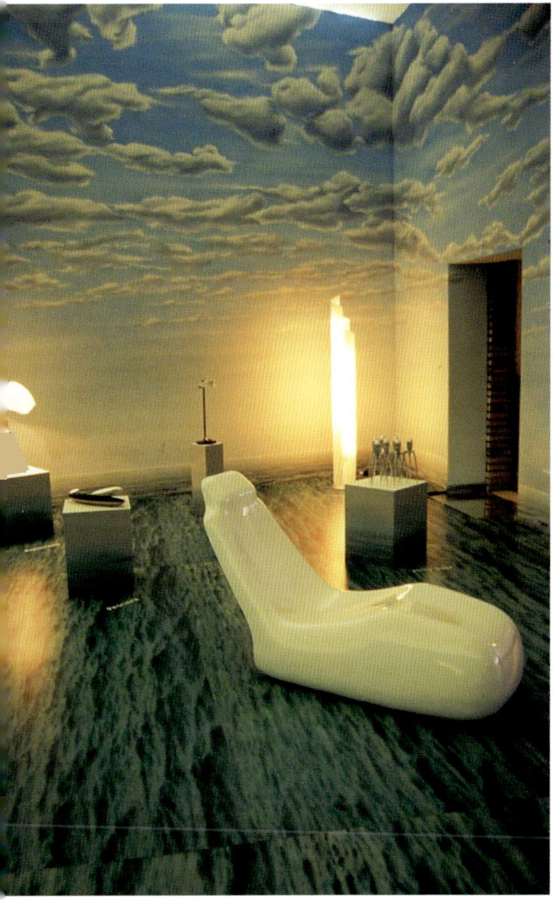

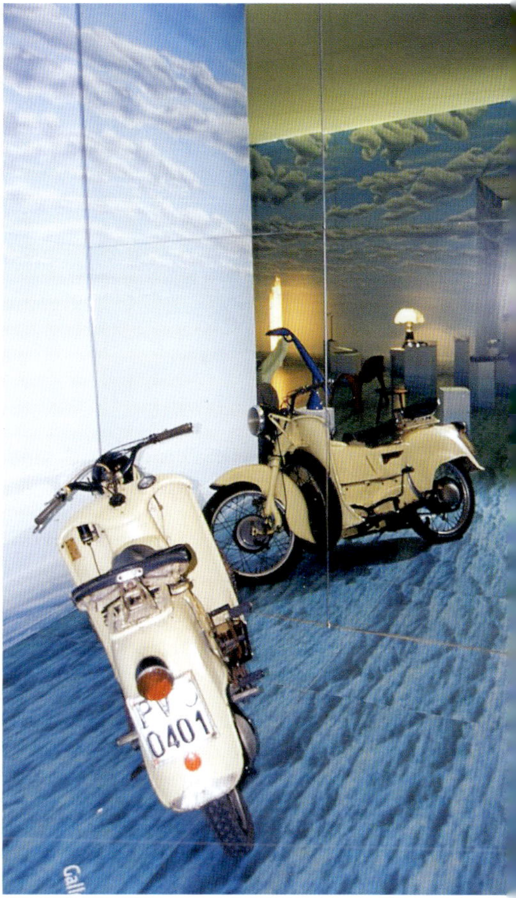

printed laminated sheets were assembled to reproduce the illusion of the rippled surface of the water.

The sky, on the other hand, was created by means of a more "hands on" technique: Gino Pelligrini, a scenery designer and decorator who has in Hollywood for fifteen years, painted on the walls a sky full of clouds that took on the forms of various animals, depending on the viewer's vantage. And so the setting was organized around the pres-

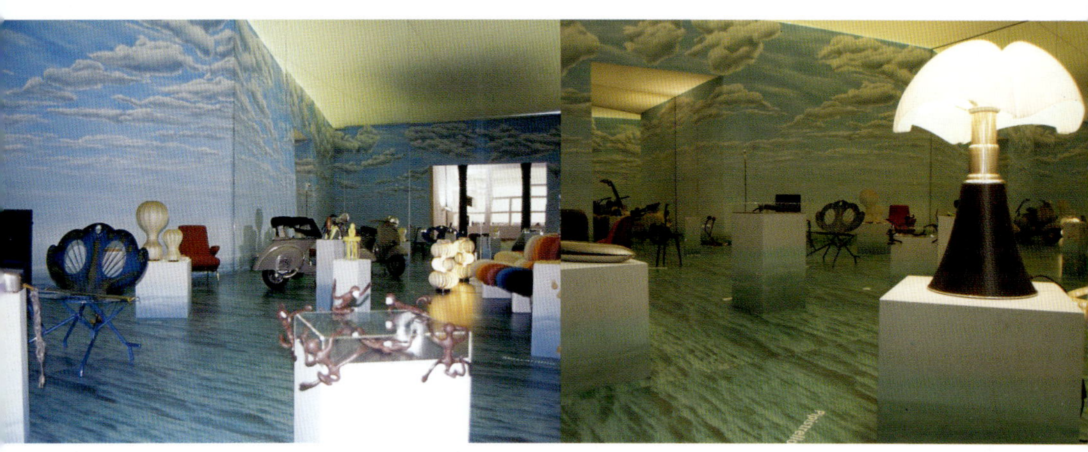

ence of opposites (technological/handcrafted), intending to create a plunging *trompe l'oeil* effect in all directions, so as to transform the specific physical space of the exhibition into a kind of macrocosm suitable for containing the "bestiary" of objects and artifacts exhibited.

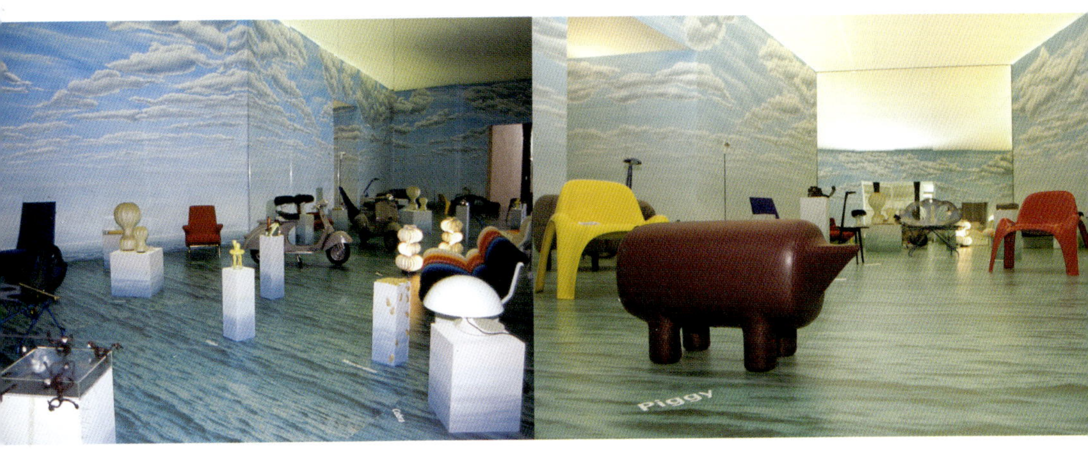

When Objects Have Animals' Names

Essential Index

16 Animali (16 Animals) · toy · 1957 · Enzo Mari · Danese
16 Pesci (16 Fish) · toy · 1973 · Enzo Mari · Danese
4 Gatti (4 Cats) · tables · 1966 · Mario Bellini · B&B Italia
Airone 250 (Heron 250) · motorcycle · 1939 · Moto Guzzi
Airone (Heron) · sofa · 1959 · Alberto Rosselli · Arflex
Airone (Heron) · lamp · 1971 · Sergio Asti · Knoll
Airone (Heron) · sofa · 2002 · Gobbi, Mazzoni Delle Stelle · Busnelli
Albatros (Albatross) · motorcycle · 1938 · Moto Guzzi
Albatros (Albatross) · lamp · 1976 · Vico Magistretti · O-Luce
Albatros (Albatross) · seat · 1976 · Titina Ammannati, Giampiero Vitelli · Brunati
Alce (Moose) · motorcycle · 1940 · Moto Guzzi
Ali-The-Gator · letter opener · 2001 · Khodi Feiz · Alessi
Anaconda · ottoman · 1999 · Ufficio Tecnico · Hivaoa
Anfibio (Amphibian) · sofa bed · 1971 · Alessandro Becchi · Giovannetti
Animali (Gli) (The Animals) · mini-drawer units · 1969 · Hans von Klier · Planula
Animali domestici (Pets) · 1985 · Andrea Branzi · Zabro
Anubis · container · 2001 · Massimo Giacon · Alessi

Ape (Bee) · vehicle · 1948 · Corradino D'Ascanio · Piaggio
Aquilotto (Eaglet) · motorcycle · 1951 · Bianchi
Balena (Whale) · soap dispenser · 2000 · Paolo Pedrizzetti · Gedy
Biancaneve (Snow White) · lamp · 1993 · Beppe Facente · Domodinamica
Bibip · lamp · 1976 · Achille Castiglioni · Flos spa
Bird · chaise lounge · 1990 · Tom Dixon · Cappellini spa
Boalum · lamp · 1969 · Livio Castiglioni, Gianfranco Frattini · Artemide
Boby · trolley · 1970 · Joe Colombo · Bieffeplast
Bollitore con l'uccellino (Kettle with Bird) · 1985 · Michael Graves · Alessi
Bruce · table cigarette-lighter · 1998 · Stefano Giovannoni · Alessi
Bruco (Caterpillar) · lamp · 1970 · Ettore Sottsass · Poltronova
Butterfly · lamp · 1985 · Afra & Tobia Scarpa · Flos
Caimano (Cayman) · prototype · 1971 · Giugiaro · Alfa Romeo
Calimero · containers · 1974 · Artigiani Comacini · Zanotta
Canguro (Kangaroo) · seat · 1970 · Giorgina Castiglioni, Giorgio Gaviraghi · Gufram
Canguro (Kangaroo) · sofa · 2000 · Terry Pecora · DNA
Cardellino 65 (Little

Goldfinch 65) · motorcycle · 1954 · Moto Guzzi
Centopiedi (Centipede) · bed · 1972 · Salmoiraghi · Kartell
Cernia (Grouper) · lamp · 1968 · Luigi Caccia Dominioni · Azucena
Chily Penguin · refrigerator thermometer · 1998 · Oscar Tusquets · Alessi
Chimera · lamp · 1966 · Vico Magistretti · Artemide
Chiocciola (Snail) · shower · 2001 · Benedini Associati · Agape
Cicalino (Little Cicada) · doormat · 1989 · Denis Santachiara · Domodinamica
Cicognino (Little Stork) · side table · 1952 · Franco Albini · Poggi
Civetta (Little Owl) · seat · 1993 · Yaacov Kaufman · Arflex
Cobra · lamp · 1968 · Elio Martinelli · Martinelli Luce
Cobra · lamp · 1974 · Luigi Caccia Dominioni · Azucena
Cobra · telephone · 1987 · Pasqui e Pasini Associati · Italtel Telematica
Coccinella (Ladybug) · prototype, seat · 1999 · Simone Micheli · MB Arredamenti Metallici
Coccodandy · holder for boiling eggs · 1998 · Stefano Giovannoni· Alessi
Colibrì (Humming-bird) · prototype, motorcycle · 1944 · Moto Guzzi
Colibrì (Humming-bird) · table ·

1976 · Michele Provinciali · Zanotta
Colibrì (Humming-bird) · bathroom series · 1995 · Ufficio Tecnico · Pozzi Ginori
Condor · motorcycle · 1937 · Moto Guzzi
Condor · seat · 1959 · Alberto Rosselli · Arflex
Coniglio Mattia (Mattia Rabbit) · electronic clock · 1998 · Mattia Di Rosa · Alessi
Cucciolo (Puppy) · bathroom fittings ·1974 · Makio Hasuike · Gedy
Delfino (Dolphin) · light motorcycle · 1951 · Motom
Delfino (Dolphin) · armchair · 1954 · Erberto Carboni · Arflex
Delfino volante (Flying Dolphin) · prototype, candlestick · 1986 · Daniele Cariani
Dingo sport · motorcycle · 1963 · Moto Guzzi
Dobermann · lamp · 1980 · Elio Martinelli · Martinelli Luce
Dobermann · skiing boots · 2000 · Nordica
Donald · lamp · 1978 · King&Mirando · Arteluce/Flos
Donald · seat · 2000 · Pierluigi Cerri · Poltrona Frau
Donald Duck · lamp · 1999 · Slamp Lab · Slamp
Dove · lamp · 1985 · Barbaglia & Colombo · Nemo Luce Italiana
Duck · lamp · 1978 · Giotto Stoppino · Candle

Duck Light · lamp · 2001 · Ernesto Gismondi · Artemide
Dumbo · faucet · 1998 · Vercelli, Marchini, Argenti · Rubinetterie Ritmonio srl
Elefante (Elephant) · soap dispenser · 2000 · Paolo Pedrizzetti · Gedy
Elefantino (Little Elephant) · 1992 · Lapo Binazzi · Eschenbach Porzellan
Escar-gogò · dish for snails · 1994 · Stefano Giovannoni · Alessi
Falco (Hawk) · motorcycle · 1987 · Moto Guzzi
Falco F8L (Hawk F8L) · light aircraft · 1960 · Stelio Frati · Aviamilano
Falcone sport (Falcon sport) · motorcycle · 1950 · Moto Guzzi
Falena (Moth) · lamp · 1968 · Mario Bellini · Candle
Falena (Moth) · lamp · 1994 · Alvaro Siza · Fontana Arte
Farfalla (Butterfly) · chair · 1953 · Conti Forlani Grassi Paoli
Farfalla (Butterfly) · seat · 1974 · Pietrantoni, Lucci, Orlandini · Elam
Fenice (Phoenix) · lamp · 1996 · Renato Toso Noti Massari & Associati · Artemide
Fido · seat · 1989 · Toshijuki Kita · Moroso
Fish Dish · 1957 · Roberto Sambonet · Sambonet
Folpo (Octopus) · beater with measure · 1998 · Marta Sansoni · Alessi

Formica (Ant) · alarm clock · 2001 · Cleto Munari · Cleto Munari
Formiche (Le) (The Ants) · lamp · 1994 · Elio Martinelli · Martinelli Luce
Fred Worm · container · 1997 · Guido Venturini · Alessi
Fritz the Cat · lamp · 1987 · King&Miranda · Arteluce/Flos
Frog · chair · 1995 · Carlo Bartoli · Ycami
Frog · suitcase · 2000 · Mambriani, Gramegna, Caramelli · Mandarina Duck
Froggy · scales · 2000 · Castiglione Morelli · Outlook Zelco Italia
Gabbiano (Seagull) · lamp · 1992 · Elio Martinelli · Martinelli Luce
Gabbiano (Seagull) · washbasin · 1994 · Giuseppe Pasquali · Agape
Galletto 160 cc (Rooster 160 cc) · motorcycle · 1950 · Carlo Guzzi · Moto Guzzi
Gatto (Cat) · lamp · 1962 · Achille Castiglioni, Pier Giacomo Castiglioni · Flos
Ghiro (Dormouse) · seat bed · 1967 · Gianfranco Masi · NY Form
Giraffa (Giraffe) · bookcase · 1960 · Paolo Tilche · Arform
Giraffa (Giraffe) · lamp · 1967 · Salvati, Tresoldi · Missaglia
Grillo (Cricket) · telephone ·1967 · Marco Zanuso · Sit Siemens
Grillo (Cricket) · motor scooter · 1990 · Giacomo Montano · Piaggio
Grillo (Cricket) · prototype,

chair · 1999 · Simone Micheli ·
MB Arredamenti Metallici
Gru (Crane) · chair · 1970 ·
Silvio Coppola · Bernini
Hebi (Snake) · lamp · 1969 ·
Isao Hosoe · Valenti
Heron · lamp · 1994 · Isao Hosoe,
Alessio Pozzoli · Luxo Italiana
Horse chair · seat · 2001 ·
Satyendra Pakhale · Cappellini spa
Iguana · prototype · 1969 ·
Giugiaro · Alfa Romeo
Ippogrifo (Hippogriff) ·
motorcycle · 1997 · Moto Guzzi
Jeti · seat · 1968 · Mario
Scheichenbauer · Elam
Juicy Salif · lemon juicer ·
1990 · Philippe Starck · Alessi
Koala · helicopter · 1994 · Agusta
Labrador · sauceboat · 1982 ·
Andrea Branzi · Memphis
Lamandarina · pen · 1998 ·
Giulio Iacchetti · Mandarina Duck
Lince 3 (Lynx 3) · camera ·
1963 · Ferrania
Lombrico (Worm) · seat ·
1967 · Marco Zanuso · B&B
Lucciola (Firefly) · lamp · 1967 ·
Salvati, Tresoldi · Missaglia
Lucciola Cinquecento (Firefly
500) · prototype · 1993 ·
Giugiaro · Italdesign
Lumaca (Snail) · lamp · 1968 ·
Umberto Riva · Fontana Arte
Lumilla · furnishing accessories ·
2000 · Laura Bartelloni · Erreti
Luxferi · seat · 1993 · Cinzia
Ruggeri · Poltrona Frau

Magic Bunny · toothpick holder ·
1998 · Stefano Giovannoni · Alessi
Manta (Manta Ray) · chair ·
1957 · Pierluigi Spadolini · ICS
Manta (Manta Ray) · prototype ·
1968 · Giugiaro · Bizzarrini
Mantis · lamp · 1978 ·
King&Miranda · Arteluce/Flos
Mariposa (Butterfly) · bench ·
1989 · Riccardo Dalisi · Zanotta
Medusa · chair · 1956 ·
Pierluigi Spadolini · ICS
Medusa · lamp · 1968 · Olaf
von Bohr · Ecolight, Valenti
Medusa · table · 1969 · Studio
Tetrarch · Bazzani
Medusa · lamp · 1977 ·
Giorgetto Giugiaro · Bilumen
Medusa · prototype · 1980 ·
Giugiaro · Lancia
Medusa · lamp · 1992 · Sergio
Asti · Salviati
Medusa · lamp · 1996 · Zanon,
Barmine, Crepax · Artemide
Meo Romeo · toy · 1949 ·
Bruno Munari · Pirelli
MG30 · cheese dish · 1997 ·
Michael Graves · Alessi
Mickey Mouse · lamp · 1998 ·
Slamp Lab · Slamp
Minnie · lamp · 1999 · Slamp
Lab · Slamp
Mister Koala · sofa · 1999 ·
Nicola Adami · Giorgetti
Mister Meumeu · cheese dish ·
1992 · Philippe Starck · Alessi
Mito di Europa (Myth of
Europe) · 1997 · Tibaldi La

Spada · Kundalini
Moby Dick · seat · 1974 ·
Alberto Rosselli · Saporiti
Moscardino (Musky Octopus) ·
fork-spoon · 2000 · Giulio
Iacchetti, Matteo Ragni ·
Pandora Design
Mosquito · motor scooter ·1946 ·
Ufficio tecnico Garelli · Garelli
Mouse · computer stand · 1998 ·
Marco Zanuso Jr · DePadova
Neolia · headboard · 1989 ·
Andrea Branzi · Zanotta
Nibbio (Kite) · motorcycle ·
1975 · Moto Guzzi
Notturno italiano (Italian
Nocturne) · lamp · 1988 ·
Denis Santachiara · Modular
Domodinamica
Nutty the Cracker ·
nutcracker · 1993 · Stefano
Giovannoni · Alessi
Orca (Killer Whale) · prototype ·
1982 · Giugiaro · Lancia
Panda · automobile · 1980 ·
Giorgetto Giugiaro · Fiat auto
Paperino (Little Gosling) ·
prototype power-assisted cycle ·
1945 · Casini & Spoldi · Industria
Meccanica Napoletana
Papero (Gosling) · lamp ·
1971 · Cini Boeri · Stilnovo
Papillon (Butterfly) · seat · 1972 ·
Guido M. Rosati · Giovannetti
Papillon (Butterfly) · thermos ·
1986 · F. Minuti · Flli Guzzini
Papillona (Butterfly) · lamp ·
1977 · Tobia Scarpa, Afra

Scarpa · Flos spa
Pavone (Peacock) · chair ·
1986 · Riccardo Dalisi · Zanotta
Pecorella (Sheep) · upholstery ·
1979 · Enzo Mari · Driade
Pecorelle (Sheep) · seats · 1979 ·
Cini Boeri, Laura Griziotti · Arflex
Pellicano (Pelican) · lamp ·
1970 · Ferrari
Penguin Tea · teapot · 1993 ·
Pierangelo Caramia · Alessi
Piggy · ottoman · 1991 · Anna
Castelli Ferrieri · Matteograssi
Pinguino pac50 (Penguin pac50) ·
air-conditioning unit · 1999 ·
Giacomo Borin Disegno industriale
De' Longhi · De' Longhi spa
Pipistrello (Bat) · lamp · 1965 ·
Gae Aulenti · Martinelli Luce
Pito · kettle · 1992 · Frank O.
Gehry · Alessi
Please Love Me · lamp ·
1998 · Riccardo Dalisi · Slamp
Pluto · chair · 1971 · De Pas,
D'Urbino, Lomazzi · BBB Bonacina
Poltrona del leone (Lion Seat) ·
seat · 1992 · Riccardo Dalisi ·
Promemoria
Pony · table · 1956 · Paolo
Tilche · Felice Rossi
Primate · seat · 1970 · Achille
and Pier Giacomo Castiglioni ·
Zanotta
Quack · adhesive tape dispenser ·
2001 · Khodi Feiz · Alessi
Reale (Royal) · table · 1946 ·
Carlo Mollino · Zanotta
Rhino · coat hook · 1998 ·

Matteo Ragni · Progetti srl
Riccio (Hedgehog) ·
centerpiece · 2000 · Johanna
Grawunder · Salviati
Rinoceronte (Rhinoceros) · drawer
unit · 1989 · Ico Parisi · Lietti
Rondine (Swallow) · camera ·
1949 · Vico D'Incerti · Ferrania
Rondini (Le) (The Swallows)·
lamp · 1984 · Elio Martinelli ·
Martinelli Luce
RSV Falco (RSV Hawk) · motor
scooter · 2001 · Longmore · Aprilia
Scarabeo (Scarab) · motor scooter ·
1993 · Ferracin Renzo · Aprilia
Seppia (Cuttlefish) · accessories ·
1988 · De Pas, D'Urbino,
Lomazzi · Tonelli
Serpello · furnishing accessories ·
2001 · Laura Bartelloni · Erreti
Serpente (Serpent) · lamp · 1965 ·
Elio Martinelli · Martinelli Luce
Serpente (Serpent) · decoration ·
1979 · Ettore Sottsass · Memphis
Serpente (Serpent) · moneybox ·
1940 · Carlo Scarpa · Venini
Serpentone (Big Snake) ·
expandable sofa · 1971 · Cini
Boeri · Arflex
Sirfo · small table · 1986 ·
Alessandro Mendini · Zanotta
Snoopy · lamp · 1967 · Achille
and Pier Giacomo Castiglioni ·
Flos
Spider · lamp · 1965 · Joe
Colombo · O-Luce
Spider · seat · 1994 · James
Irvine · Cappellini spa

Tapira (Tapir) · lamp · 1974 ·
Gianemilio, Piero & Anna
Monti · Fontana Arte
Tartaruga (Tortoise) · cable
telephony receiver · 1957 ·
Roberto Menghi · Sit Siemens
The Fly · drawing pins · 2001 ·
Donata Paruccini · Alessi
Topo (Mouse) · lamp · 1970 ·
Joe Colombo · Stilnovo Italia
Topolino 500 (Little Mouse
500) · automobile · 1936 ·
Dante Giacosa · Fiat
Topolino (Little Mouse) · lamp ·
1989 · Matteo Thun · Studio Thun
Topolone (Big Mouse) · sofa ·
1981 · Massimo Morozzi · Edra
Tortue (Tortoise) · lamp · 1975 ·
Rodolfo Bonetto · Candle
Tropical · bathmat · 2001 ·
Marina Paul, Francesco
Scansetti · Outlook Zelco Italia
Turtle · seat · 2002 · Giorgio
Cugliari, Stefano Corò · Reverse
Vespa 98 cc (Wasp 98 cc) ·
motor scooter · 1946 ·
Corradino D'Ascanio · Piaggio
Zabro (Ground Beetle) · chair-
table · 1984 · Alessandro
Mendini · Zanotta
Zefiro (Zephyr) · lamp · 1992 ·
Riccardo Dalisi · O-Luce
Zigolo (Bunting) · motorcycle ·
1953 · Moto Guzzi
Zizì · toy · 1952 · Bruno
Munari · Pirelli

We thank the followings
Alessi · Arflex · Artemide ·
B&B · Cini Boeri · Cappellini ·
Giorgina Castiglioni ·
Carlo Civardi · Flos ·
Fontana Arte · Galleria del
Design e dell'Arredamento
Cantù · Giovannetti ·
Gufram · Luxo Italiana ·
Martinelli Luce ·
Matteograssi · Modular
Domodinamica · Pandora
Design · Anty Pansera ·
Pietro Pedrini · Poggi ·
Giovanna Ponti · Rosselli ·
Valenti · Zanotta

**For their kind
collaboration**
Francesca Appiani ·
Archivio storico Moto
Guzzi · Archivio storico
Piaggio · Liliana Bondoni ·
Gianluca Borgesi · Anna
Castelli Ferrieri · Riccardo
Dalisi · Isao Hosoe · Simona
Maspero · King & Miranda ·
Giulio Iacchetti · Poltrona
Frau

and also
Enrico Mastrapasqua ·
Matteo Ragni · Roberto
Rizzi · Paola Romano ·
Paolo Rosselli · Giovanna
Solinas · Beppe Utano

Photographic Credits

Archivio fotografico della Triennale di Milano,
Ph. di Amendolagine e Barracchia:
pp. 46, 48 (in alto), 50 (in basso), 54 (a sinistra), 61,
62 (in alto), 71, 72, 75 (a sinistra), 77, 81, 95

Archivio Albini p. 74
Archivio Alessi pp. 64 (in alto ph.Studio Azzurro; in
basso schizzo Frank O. Gehry), 65, 67(schizzo di
Khodi Feiz), 83, 98, 99 (ph. S. Kirchner)
Archivio Artemide pp. 50 (in alto), 89
Archivio B&B p. 45
Archivio Cappellini p. 80
Archivio Anna Castelli Ferrieri p. 57 (in alto a sinistra,
ph. François Robert)
Archivio Cini Boeri pp. 55, 76 (ph. Aldo Ballo)
Archivio Flos pp. 47, 91
Archivio Fontana Arte p. 82
Archivio Galleria dell'Arredamento Cantù pp. 86, 87
Archivio Giorgina Castiglioni pp. 53
Archivio Isao Hosoe p. 52
Archivio King&Miranda p. 96 (ph. Andrea Zani)
Archivio Martinelli Luce p. 49
Archivio Matteograssi p. 56 (ph. Beppe Raso)
Archivio Modular Domodinamica p. 97
Archivio Moto Guzzi p. 73
Archivio Rosselli pp. 92, 93
Archivio Valenti p. 63
Archivio Zanotta pp. 51, 78, 94
Riccardo Dalisi, disegni, p. 79
Studio Iacchetti Ragni p. 66, fotografia e disegno

Carosello. Non è vero che tutto fa brodo. 1957-1977,
Silvana Editore 1996 p. 137, p. 94 in alto
"Domus" n° 452, luglio 1967, p. 75 in alto

Printed in September 2002
by La Grafica-Cantù, e-mail: lagrafica@cracantu.it
for Edizioni Charta